The Sixties

An illustrated
History in colour
1960-1970

By
Nathaniel Harris

Special Adviser:
Dr J M Roberts
Fellow and Tutor in Modern History
at Merton College, Oxford

Macdonald Educational

The Sixties

Contents

4   The Cuban Crisis
6   The Berlin Wall
8   The Kennedy Years
10 The Africa: the Wind of Change
12 The Commonwealth
14 The Swinging Sixties
16 Fashion: The Young Idea
18 China: the Cultural Revolution
20 Sport in the Sixties
22 Europe United?
24 De Gaulle's France
26 The Six Day War
28 Czechoslovakia Invaded
30 The Third World
32 Vietnam
34 Entertainment and Leisure
36 America in Turmoil
38 Transport and Travel
40 Science
42 Space Exploration
44 The Cost of Affluence
46 The Arts
48 The End of the Cold War?
50 The Permissive Society
52 Protest!
54 The Main Events
56 Who Was Who
58 Project: Man and the Moon
60 Project: Op Art
62 Index
64 Further Reading and Acknowledgements

© 1973 Macdonald Educational Ltd.
Macdonald & Co. (Publishers) Ltd.
Maxwell House, Worship Street,
London EC2A 2 EN

Hardback Edition
First published 1975
Reprinted 1978, 1981, 1983, 1984, 1986

ISBN 0-382-06098-9

Library of Congress Catalog
Card Number 75-18048

Published in the United States by
Silver Burdett Company,
Morristown, New Jersey
Printed in the United States

◄ **Russia invades Czechoslovakia**—and a boy vainly waves the Czech flag over a Russian tank.

The sixties brought remarkable changes—in politics, in ways of living, even in beliefs.

The gradual improvement in relations between the U.S.A. and Russia made it seem that a world-destroying nuclear war might yet be avoided. Both "superpowers" were less confident than in the fifties. Russia had quarrelled bitterly with her ally China, and found it hard to keep the leadership of the Communist world. In turn, the U.S. became demoralised by its long, painful struggle in Vietnam.

Europe prospered, though still divided between East and West. Her ex-colonies swelled the ranks of the "Third World", most of them lagging badly behind the wealthy industrial nations. Ironically, high production itself created a problem, because of the damaging effects of industrial waste.

In the West, a "youth revolution" took place in dress, music and values, and accepted ideas about sex, politics and religion were challenged. Young people also took a leading part in the political unrest that swept over much of the world.

Unrest often led to violence. In fact the growth of violence was a disturbing feature of the sixties; even traditionally peaceful societies suffered from the effects of crime, riots, civil wars or military take-overs.

Against this background, the landing of men on the Moon—possibly a turning point in history—was a heartening confirmation that men could still achieve miracles of co-operative effort.

▲ **"Flower people" or hippies** at a pop concert. The beards and long hair, kaftans, beads, sandals, etc. represented a radical break with Western conventions of dress. And in fact the hippie "underground" rejected the Western way of life (concerned with money, success, technology, war) and proclaimed itself an "alternative society". It favoured simple communal living, free experiment with drugs and sex, and a commitment to "peace and love"; the slogan "flower power" emphasised a non-violent outlook by contrast with, e.g., Black Power. Open-air pop festivals lasted several days and often attracted thousands.

The attitude of hippies affected other youth. The need to achieve—at least in terms of material success—did not seem to drive them as it had their parents. Perhaps this was because the affluence of a fortunate "First World" made it easier to "do their own thing"

The Cuban Crisis

Revolution in Cuba brought the first Communist government in the Americas – and almost led on to a nuclear war.

In the fifties Cuba was a dictatorship under General Fulgencio Batista. Thanks to her sugar industry, much of it U.S.-owned, she was fairly prosperous, but Batista was unpopular, and Cubans resented "Yankee" influence on their country.

In 1956 Fidel Castro landed in eastern Cuba with only eighty followers, determined to use guerrilla tactics to defeat the well-equipped Cuban army. Batista tried to crush the rebels in their mountain bases, where they had won the support of the peasants, but failed disastrously.

Finally, in January 1959, Batista fled and Castro took power. His reforms included the nationalisation of huge areas of land owned by U.S. companies, to which the U.S. replied by refusing to buy Cuban sugar.

Then Russia stepped in to aid Cuba, and Castro nationalised all the main industries. Convinced that Castro was moving towards Communism, the U.S. government encouraged and helped anti-Castro exiles to land a force in Cuba at the Bay of Pigs (April 1961). The expedition received no popular support and was soon forced to surrender. A few months later, Castro openly declared his Communist beliefs.

▲ **Fidel Castro** making a speech. Castro was a lawyer before turning to revolutionary politics. In 1953 he led an attack on a Cuban army barracks for which he was imprisoned for twenty-two months. Then he left Cuba for Mexico, where he trained his guerrillas. After their victory, he and his men kept the beards and battledress they had worn in the mountains, as a sign that they were not going to be corrupted by power.

▶ **Cuban Communism** was not created by the orthodox Communist Party but by Castro's 26th July Movement, here glorified at a great public rally. Castro later merged the two parties into a new Communist Party under his own leadership. His independent attitude was equally clear in his dealings with Russia: though Cuba needed Russia as a customer for her sugar, Castro acted as an ally but not a stooge, refusing to copy or obey the Russians.

Conflict in Cuba

The Cuban missile crisis brought the world closer to nuclear war than ever before. In October 1962 the United States discovered that the Russians had been sending rockets and jet planes to Cuba, and setting up missile-launching sites there. To Americans, already angered by the existence of a Communist state a few miles from Florida, this was an outrageous threat; to the Cubans, who had just beaten off the Bay of Pigs invasion, it seemed a necessary defence against U.S. aggression.

President Kennedy announced a U.S. "quarantine", which meant that the American navy would stop arms shipments from reaching Cuba. The Russians decided not to risk war by forcing their way through, and Kennedy and the Russian leader Khrushchev began to confer through the United Nations.

The dramatic settlement they reached was a defeat for Russia, who had to withdraw the missiles and dismantle the bases. But in return the United States did agree not to attack Cuba or aid anti-Castro rebels.

Peace demonstrations were held in many Western countries. These were mainly in protest against the United States' willingness to risk war — especially since the U.S. had its own missile bases near Russia's border, in Turkey. The outcome of the crisis did show that both East and West wanted to avoid war; and it marked a turning point in the history of the Cold War.

▲ **Ernesto "Che" Guevara** was an Argentinian who joined Castro's rebellion and became one of the leaders of the new Cuba. Convinced that all South America was ripe for revolution, Guevara left Cuba to lead a small band of guerrillas in Bolivia. After his capture and execution by the Bolivian army, he became a romantic martyr in the eyes of many radicals, and especially to young people.

◄ **"Bolivia shall not be another Cuba"**, proclaims this poster, with its grim picture of revolutionary violence. The Bolivian peasants gave Che Guevara little support, and in the sixties guerrillas were no more successful in other South American countries. In most parts of the continent, it was the army, not revolutionaries or "the people", that succeeded in taking power.

The Berlin Wall

Germany had been divided ever since 1945. The most uncertain factor in the situation was the old capital, Berlin.

East Germany had developed from the Russian-occupied zone after World War II and belonged to the Communist bloc. West Germany was a member of N.A.T.O. and other Western alliances. Though talks were held about unification, most people realised that this division of Germany was permanent.

The fate of Berlin, deep in East Germany, was still at issue. The city was also divided—making the non-Communist part, West Berlin, a Western outpost in the Communist world. Under wartime treaties there were still Western (and Russian) troops in the city. And—worst of all from the Communist point of view—West Berlin served as a place of refuge for fleeing East Germans, more than two million of whom eventually reached the West in this way.

From 1958 the Russian leader, Khrushchev, put pressure on the West to end the wartime agreements—which would mean the withdrawal of all foreign troops. Believing this would simply leave West Berlin at the mercy of East Germany, the West refused, standing firm even when the Russians seemed to be threatening war.

Then the Communists changed their tactics. Overnight, on the 12th-13th August 1961, the East Germans sealed off West Berlin behind a brick-and-barbed-wire barrier—the "Berlin Wall".

The West protested that this broke the wartime agreements, but accepted the situation, though American troops were sent to protect West Berlin.

"The Wall" imprisoned the East Germans but cooled off the crisis. It became the latest feature of the now-established division of Germany.

▶ **One of the first casualties of the Wall** is carried away by East German guards. After August 1961 there were few successful escapes.

▲ **American school in West Germany.** The presence of U.S. and other Western forces increased Russian and East German suspicions of West Germany—in spite of the fact that there were massive Russian forces stationed in Eastern Europe. Russia had suffered terribly in World War Two, and had a genuine fear that Nazism and German aggression might reappear. At the same time, the German "threat" was used by Russian propaganda to gain sympathisers in the West and keep the East European states faithful to the Russian alliance.

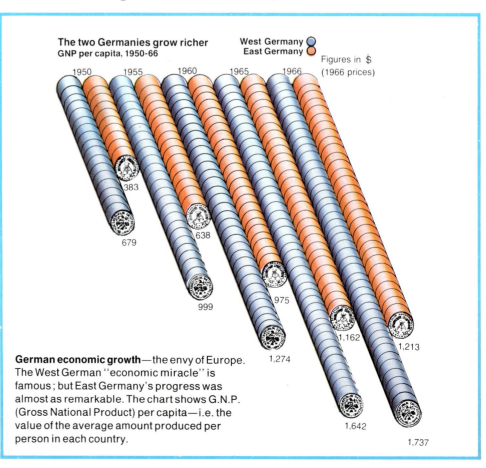

The two Germanies grow richer
GNP per capita, 1950-66

West Germany 🔵
East Germany 🟠
Figures in $ (1966 prices)

1950 · 1955 · 1960 · 1965 · 1966

383
679
638
999
975
1,274
1,162
1,213
1,642
1,737

German economic growth—the envy of Europe. The West German "economic miracle" is famous; but East Germany's progress was almost as remarkable. The chart shows G.N.P. (Gross National Product) per capita—i.e. the value of the average amount produced per person in each country.

The Kennedy Years

In November 1960, Americans elected a young, dynamic president who promised an era of action and reform. But less than three years later he had been shot down by an assassin.

The fifties had been a period of prosperity and conservative government under President Eisenhower. Kennedy stood for a more active policy, including measures to stamp out poverty and racial prejudice, and an ambitious space programme to catch up with the Russians.

In practice, much of Kennedy's time was given to foreign affairs. Shortly before his election, the Russians had shot down an American U-2 spy plane over their territory, and as a result the East-West summit meeting in Paris had broken down. The Cold War seemed as bitter as ever.

Kennedy's policy combined firmness with a willingness to come to terms with Russia and her allies. He made a bad mistake in backing an invasion of Cuba (page 5), but he handled the Cuban missile crisis in such a way that though Russia gave way she was not humiliated. Similarly, he supported West Berlin but did not try to stop the building of the Berlin Wall.

Better East-West relations were signalled by the "hot line"—a direct telephonic link installed between the U.S.A. and U.S.S.R. after the Cuban crisis.

At home, Kennedy's policies were less successful. Most of his welfare and civil rights schemes were blocked by Congress, though many were later put through by the next president, L. B. Johnson—who also inherited a disastrous Vietnam policy.

What Kennedy himself might have done cannot be known. Suddenly, in mid-career, he was struck down by an assassin's bullets while driving through Dallas, Texas. The assassination shook the world, and began a violent, turbulent period in the U.S.

◄ **A rapturous welcome for Kennedy** in Mexico. His good looks, charm, wealth and political skill swept him to the presidency at the early age of 43, despite the supposed disadvantage of being a Catholic.

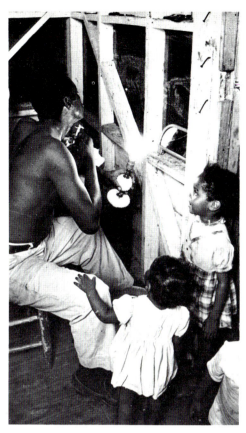

▲ **Negro living conditions remained poor** in affluent America. Northern slums were hardly better than Southern shanties in this respect. Conservatives and Southerners in Congress blocked many of Kennedy's reforms.

▶ **Kennedy in West Berlin,** 1963. His famous "Ich bin ein Berliner!" ("I am a Berliner!") speech expressed his sympathy with the city's difficult situation. With him is Willy Brandt, then mayor of West Berlin.

▼ **Kennedy's assassination** remained something of a mystery, since the assassin was himself killed shortly afterwards. Kennedy's widow, Jackie, appears here with his brother Robert—himself murdered in 1968.

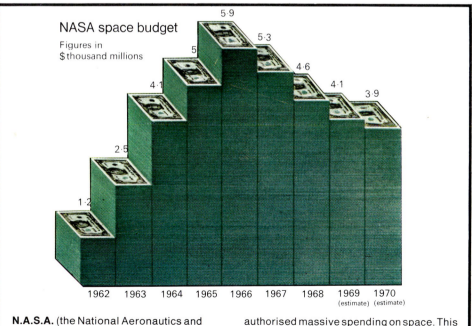

NASA space budget
Figures in $ thousand millions

1962 — 1·2
1963 — 2·5
1964 — 4·1
1965 — 5
1966 — 5·9
1967 — 5·3
1968 — 4·6
1969 (estimate) — 4·1
1970 (estimate) — 3·9

N.A.S.A. (the National Aeronautics and Space Administration) was an organisation set up in 1958 to take charge of the U.S. space programme. But it was Kennedy who authorised massive spending on space. This prepared the way for later U.S. triumphs, though critics argued that it used up resources more urgently needed on Earth.

Africa: the Wind of Change

▲ **The Congo crisis** began when the Belgians left in 1960. Years of army mutinies and massacres followed. The country seemed likely to fall apart when copper-rich Katanga tried to break away (the photo shows Katangan miners). U.N. troops restored some order.

In 1960 most of Africa was still ruled by Europeans; by 1970 almost the entire continent consisted of independent states.

Having once made up their minds, Britain, France and Belgium quitted Africa with astounding speed. This was the "wind of change" described by the British Prime Minister, Harold Macmillan, in a famous speech. With Africa south of the Sahara rapidly falling under black African control, the days of white minority rule in the south—Angola, Mozambique, South Africa, Rhodesia —seemed numbered.

But the seeming strength and unity of the new Africa proved an illusion. African states developed the same rivalries as states elsewhere, and most of their governments felt—and were—insecure.

The colonial powers had given the African peoples little political training, and in many places the tribe—not the nation—was the focus of loyalty. Such conditions, combined with economic backwardness, did not favour peaceful development, and the sixties were a period of political upheaval.

The greatest tragedies were terrible civil wars in the Congo and Nigeria, triggered off by tribal jealousies. The political trend was right away from the parliamentary systems set up by the colonial powers: either the ruling party banned its rivals and set up a one-party state, or the army seized power. The future of the continent remained uncertain.

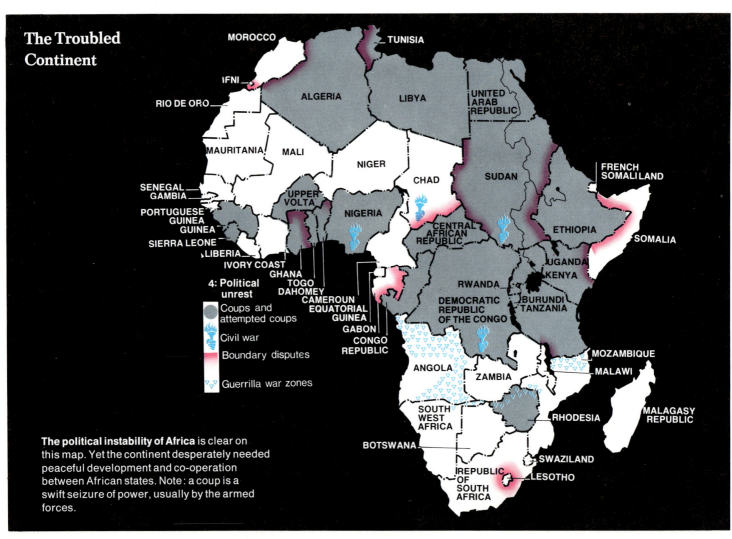

The Troubled Continent

4: Political unrest

⬤ Coups and attempted coups

Civil war

Boundary disputes

▽ Guerrilla war zones

The political instability of Africa is clear on this map. Yet the continent desperately needed peaceful development and co-operation between African states. Note: a coup is a swift seizure of power, usually by the armed forces.

MOROCCO · TUNISIA · IFNI · RIO DE ORO · ALGERIA · LIBYA · UNITED ARAB REPUBLIC · MAURITANIA · MALI · NIGER · CHAD · SUDAN · FRENCH SOMALILAND · SENEGAL · GAMBIA · PORTUGUESE GUINEA · GUINEA · UPPER VOLTA · NIGERIA · CENTRAL AFRICAN REPUBLIC · ETHIOPIA · SOMALIA · SIERRA LEONE · LIBERIA · IVORY COAST · GHANA · TOGO · DAHOMEY · CAMEROUN · EQUATORIAL GUINEA · GABON · CONGO REPUBLIC · UGANDA · KENYA · RWANDA · BURUNDI · TANZANIA · DEMOCRATIC REPUBLIC OF THE CONGO · ANGOLA · ZAMBIA · MOZAMBIQUE · MALAWI · SOUTH WEST AFRICA · BOTSWANA · RHODESIA · MALAGASY REPUBLIC · SWAZILAND · REPUBLIC OF SOUTH AFRICA · LESOTHO

► **Independence celebrations.** Scenes like this one (in Tanzania) took place over most of Africa in the sixties. But joy was often followed by disillusion as independence failed to solve the problems of poverty and backwardness. African leaders were not necessarily more efficient and honest than the Europeans they had replaced—or than the national army, which often came to the conclusion that it could run things better.

▼ **Biafran sergeant and his men.** The Nigerian civil war illustrated the dangers of tribalism. The people of eastern Nigeria, the Ibo, worked and traded all over the country. Other tribes resented their success, and in 1966 there were massacres of Ibo that made thousands flee to the east. The Ibo set up their own state, Biafra; but the Nigerian government reconquered the breakaway—after four horrible years of war, famine and disease.

Kwame Nkrumah led the first successful independence movement in modern Africa. In 1957 the British Gold Coast became independent Ghana, with Nkrumah as Prime Minister. This began the "wind of change". Nkrumah set up a one-party state, overthrown by the army in 1966.

Julius K. Nyerere was the first Prime Minister of Tanganyka, which became independent in 1961, and first President when it became a republic in 1962. In 1964 Tanganyka and Zanzibar united to form Tanzania, a one-party "African socialist" state under Nyerere's leadership.

The Commonwealth

By the end of the sixties, the old British Empire had completed its transformation into a multiracial Commonwealth.

▲ **South African pass-book:** an identity card compulsory for all blacks. South Africa's racial policies led to her leaving the Commonwealth in 1961.

▶ **White domination in Rhodesia:** a cartoonist's view of Prime Minister Ian Smith and his white supporters. Rather than accept African majority rule, Smith declared Rhodesia independent, defying British and world pressure.

▼ **The passing of the British Empire** left the "mother country" unsure of her future destiny. This was reflected in the satire of the sixties, which mocked Britain's leaders with a new ferocity ("Bloody Harold" is Harold Wilson).

After World War II, a whole series of Britain's African, Asian and West Indian colonies gained their independence. Most of them decided to remain in the Commonwealth, joining older members like Australia, whose populations were mainly of European descent.

The Commonwealth was a friendly association, not a power bloc. As such, it showed that peoples of different races and religions could discuss problems and work together. On the other hand, some British hopes for the Commonwealth were disappointed in the sixties. For example, western-style parliaments failed to survive in some countries, giving way to one-party states or military rule. Commonwealth nations often suffered from the same kind of problems and strains as other countries.

Although the Commonwealth was a multi-racial organization, racial problems troubled it. South Africa formally left the Commonwealth, and the Rhodesian Government broke off relations with Britain. In both countries, policy favoured white domination.

Many Black African states penalized their Asian citizens; in particular the Indians who formed the trading class. In Britain itself there was racial ill-feeling as immigrants from the West Indies and Pakistan—many of them British passport holders—arrived in great numbers.

Other political problems were tribal rivalries in Africa, which flared into civil war in Nigeria (page 11); geography, which split Pakistan in two; and nationalism, which caused even long-settled Canada to suffer the pangs of a separatist movement in Quebec.

Empire and Commonwealth

INDEPENDENCE 1966

35 CENTS

35 CENTS

G. SOBERS, B'DOS & W.I. CAPTAIN

BARBADOS

Map labels:

NEW ZEALAND
Cook Is.
TONGA
New Hebrides
Macquarie Is.
WESTERN SAMOA
Fiji Is.
British Solomon Is.
Territory of Papua
Cayman Is.
JAMAICA
British Honduras
Turks and Caicos Is.
Bahamas
Gilbert and Ellice Is.
NAURU
New Ireland
New Britain
Trust Territory of New Guinea
UNITED STATES OF AMERICA
CANADA
SINGAPORE
Windward Is.
Bermuda
Leeward Is.
BARBADOS
TRINIDAD and TOBAGO
GUYANA
AUSTRALIA
Falkland Is.
South Georgia
Hongkong
EIRE
PAKISTAN
Gibraltar
CYPRUS ISRAEL
INDIA
BURMA
MALAYSIA
South Sandwich
St. Helena
SUDAN
CEYLON
GAMBIA
MALTA
MALDIVES
SIERRA LEONE
UNITED ARAB REPUBLIC
SOUTHERN YEMEN
Ascension I.
GHANA
KENYA
Seychelles
Tristan da Cunha
NIGERIA
UGANDA
SOMALILAND PROTECTORATE
SOUTH CAMEROONS
TANZANIA
Rhodesia
Mauritius
SOUTH WEST AFRICA
SOUTH AFRICA
MALAWI
Swaziland
BOTSWANA
LESOTHO
ZAMBIA

- (green) Dependency of the U.K., Australia or New Zealand
- (blue) Independent Commonwealth country recognizing the Sovereign as head of state
- (olive) Independent Commonwealth country not recognizing the Sovereign as head of state
- (yellow) Former British mandate or territory now outside the Commonwealth

The following countries became independent during the sixties, staying in the Commonwealth:

Nigeria (1960)
Sierra Leone; Tanzania (1961)
Uganda; Jamaica; Trinidad and Tobago; Western Samoa (1962)
Kenya (1963)
Malawai; Zambia (1964)
The Gambia (1965)
Guyana; Barbados;
Botswana; Lesotho (1966)
Swaziland (1968)

Rhodesia declared herself independent in 1965 and a republic in 1970; South Yemen became independent and left the Commonwealth in 1967.

▲ **India's Mrs Indira Gandhi**, Prime Minister from 1966. Poverty, overpopulation and economic backwardness were India's chief enemies, and progress in defeating them was painfully slow in spite of foreign aid. Border skirmishes with China led to Chinese retaliation (1962), and long-standing quarrels with Pakistan broke out into a brief war (1965).

▶ **Elections in Pakistan.** Political rights were limited after General Ayub Khan took over, though an attempt was made to build local democracy. Pakistan's greatest problem was the division of the country into two areas a thousand miles apart. In 1971, after bitter civil war, East Pakistan broke away to form a new state, Bangladesh.

The Swinging Sixties

In the West, there was an air of glamour and excitement about the sixties. And, thanks to prosperity, a greater number of people were able to share in "the good life."

▲ **Beatniks** appeared in America during the fifties, and also made some impact on Europe. Like later groups they "dropped out" of conventional society, admired Zen Buddhism and other Eastern religions, and were strongly influenced by music (mainly modern jazz). But whereas beatniks were a small minority, millions were influenced by Sixties "Flower Power".

Teenagers now had a good deal of money to spend, and so manufacturers began to make records, clothes and other goods especially for them.

Affluence encouraged greater independence, and so did "permissiveness" (page 50). Instead of copying older people, the young developed their own "culture", centred on various forms of pop music. The old adult standards—of quiet, neat dressing and restrained behaviour—gave way to a taste for extravagance and colour.

For much of the sixties Britain seemed the most "swinging" of all countries. The Beatles and other British groups dominated pop music, and cheap, imaginative and colourful British clothes were copied throughout the West.

At this time, the Swinging Sixties seemed mainly about fun and freedom.

The hippies of the later sixties were a sign of a new mood. They rejected society's values and believed in "dropping out"—refusing to take part in the "rat race" for jobs and money. And from this a whole "Underground" or "counter-culture" developed.

Only a minority did drop out, and for many people the "counter-culture" was a fashion rather than something they believed in deeply. But through thousands of "part-time" hippies the underground had a wide influence.

Confidence in the programme of "peace and love" tended to wane, especially in America, during the long campaign against the Vietnam war. Militant political action turned many young people to the New Left (page 52)—a far cry from the carefree atmosphere of the early "Swinging Sixties".

▲ **The Beatles,** easily the most famous pop group of the sixties. Here they are showing the decorations awarded to them for services to music and the export trade. (The sale of their records abroad brought badly needed foreign currency to Britain.) Later, like many others, they adopted far less conventional clothes and attitudes.

▲ **Beatlemania.** Screaming, weeping and fainting fans were nothing new: girls had "swooned" at the slow ballads sung by Frank Sinatra in the forties. But part of the appeal of the Beatles, and others, was that they seemed "ordinary"—though their continuing success was partly the result of genuinely original talent, especially for songwriting.

▲ **Dancing at a disco.** The discothèque was a new form of dance hall. Instead of "live" music, records were played on powerful stereos.

▼ **Pop records** were sold by the million, mainly to young people; and it was typical of the sixties' mood that older people tended to follow the trends set by the young.

▲ **The new mood** of the late sixties carried over into the next decade. Buskers, street markets, antique stalls, long skirts and bell-bottom trousers all began their long reign in the sixties. Under twenty-five became a magic age, and young people the world over were united by this simplest of bonds. Pop music crossed political frontiers, as did fashions. Non-conformity was the creed of the young.

▲ **Hippie selling "underground" newspapers** at Haight-Ashbury. This was a district of San Francisco in which hippies gathered, creating a "counter-culture" with its own styles, customs and newspapers. It was imitated all over the West.

Fashion: the Young Idea

Carnaby Street, just off Regent Street, London, was one of the most famous places in Europe during the sixties. The original, smart and relatively cheap clothes in its boutiques soon made it one of Britain's major tourist attractions.

The Portobello Road, in West London, became one of the city's busiest markets, crowded with stalls and small shops. New and second-hand clothes were for sale, including many "fun" clothes such as old military uniforms.

▶ **The "leggy look"** came in with the mini-skirt, which outdid even the short skirts of the "roaring twenties". The most admired type of figure was long-legged and ultra-slim, though not, generally speaking, so slim as the model shown here—Twiggy, who nonetheless went on to become a popular film and T.V. performer.

Fashions changed rapidly in the sixties, reflecting a sense of liberation from formal styles.

Fashion had always been controlled by the great Parisian designers. Their elaborate, luxurious clothes were intended for wealthy customers, but were copied all over the West in cheaper materials; other clothes for ordinary people were simply basic, unstylish "ready-mades".

In the sixties, all this changed. Young, unknown designers began to make clothes for the young and not-so-wealthy. Their emphasis on gaiety, colour and sex-appeal matched the mood of the sixties, and little shops called boutiques sprang up everywhere, selling cheap, adventurously designed clothes—for men as well as for women.

Many of the new designers were British, and Mary Quant, Ossie Clark and others soon became internationally known. Ventures which began in cheap rooms in Carnaby Street, London, became important companies, and the new styles began to be mass-produced for ready-to-wear clothing.

With the mini-skirt, showing several inches of thigh above the knee, the dress revolution was in full swing. Later styles ranged from the full-length maxi-skirt to various "unisex" outfits which could be worn by male and female alike.

The keynote of all these styles was informality. This tendency reached a climax in the hippie styles popular in the late sixties among young people. Though there were "fashions", there had never been such a display of originality and variety in dress.

▲ **Hippie designers.** Their clothes are smart versions of hippie fashions in 1967. The vaguely "eastern" look, the soft, velvety materials and embroidery, and the colourful jewellery, are all fairly typical.

    This style completed the revolution in men's appearance. In leisure time, at least, the traditional drabness and formality gave way to bright colours and casual comfort. Hair was worn long for the first time in sixty years. And, in general, men were happy to look much less "masculine".

▲ **Plastic macs,** yellow PVCs and bright, utilitarian, easy-care fabrics were the hallmark of sixties' ready-to-wear.

▲ **The gangster look** made its appearance in the late sixties. The film *Bonnie and Clyde*—and a general cult of the twenties—made it popular. Another influence was *Dr Zhivago,* which started a vogue for "Russian" clothes such as fur hats and long heavy overcoats.

▲ **"Mods" dancing.** Youth fashions in Britain had developed into rival styles by the mid-sixties. "Rockers" wore leather jackets and other gear suitable for riding massive "ton-up" motorcycles. Tough and functional, the style carried on, and was adopted by the Hell's Angels. "Mods" were strikingly different with their short haircuts and general neatness. Notice the leather jacket, crew-neck jumper and elastic-sided boots in the photo; also the girl's skirt, still calf-length. There were often gang fights between Mods and Rockers.

China: the Cultural Revolution

▲ **Liu Shao-ch'i** had succeeded Mao as President of China in 1959. He was the most important victim of the Cultural Revolution.

▼ **The Chinese army,** guided by the "little red book", firmly supported Mao in the sixties.

Apparently strong and stable, China was almost torn apart by the "Great Proletarian Cultural Revolution."

By the early sixties China seemed to be settling down after the 1949 Communist Revolution. As in Russia, the Communist Party was firmly in control, and a centralised state-directed economy began to develop.

But Mao, who had led the revolution, was determined to make China live up to the Communist ideal of a society owned and run by the workers—unlike Russia, in practice controlled from the top by a Communist Party elite. Launching the 1966 Cultural Revolution, he soon swept aside all opposition.

Mao began the Cultural Revolution by encouraging a massive public campaign of criticism, directed against teachers, party leaders, and other authorities. Students were formed into Red Guards who travelled all over China, tearing down signs and monuments linked with the old Chinese tradition. Officials high and low were put on trial and made to confess their "errors". Revolutionary committees took over part of the work—and power —of the Communist Party.

Mao himself gained a god-like authority. Millions carried the "little red book" of *Thoughts of Chairman Mao*.

The Cultural Revolution badly upset the course of government, education and industry, and in many areas the army had to move in and restore order. Eventually the over-enthusiastic Red Guards were disbanded, and by 1968-9, life was returning to normal.

▲ **News and propaganda** put out by the Red Guards in Canton. The Chinese use posters as a cheap, eye-catching form of newspaper—which millions can read, thanks to a successful campaign against illiteracy.

▶ **The new leaders of China,** Mao believed, must not lose touch with the people. Trained political workers (like the ones shown here) are expected to do their share in the fields or on the factory floor.

The New China

In Mao's China the people are supposed to be involved in decision-making at every level. The country is divided into communes which run their own affairs; the people of a commune are in charge of the education in their area, and they decide what goods should be produced and marketed.

In most countries—both dictatorships and democracies—the common man is a stranger to the actual workings of his government; so Mao's China is a great political experiment. But the Maoist personality cult, chanted slogans in mass meetings, military-style marches and intolerance of opposition, are less attractive sides of life in the new China.

During the sixties, China was largely shut off from the outside world. She had quarrelled with her Russian allies, whom she thought too "soft" towards the United States. In turn, U.S. influence kept China out of the United Nations.

Isolation increased the traditional Chinese suspicion of foreigners. At the same time, China was becoming stronger. She built up her industries without outside help, and manufactured her own atomic and hydrogen bombs.

◀ **Red Guards** attacking writers who have criticised Mao. The Cultural Revolution placed the "common good" above personal choice.

Sport in the Sixties

Sport in the sixties was highly professional, glamorous, and often big business. Many leading sportsmen had the same sort of following as pop stars.

Scientific training methods and better facilities helped sportsmen to achieve peak fitness. Records were broken regularly, greatly adding to the spectator appeal of most sports.

Sport became increasingly professional. Amateurs were no longer able to compete with full-time players trained by modern methods. One casualty was cricket's annual Gentlemen versus Players match—i.e. amateurs versus professionals—which had to be abandoned.

For the gifted player, the lure of high money rewards made turning professional irresistably attractive. Significantly, the dominance of professionals in tennis led to a decline in the prestige of the famous Wimbledon tournament—until it was thrown open to professionals in 1968. Even where professionalism was forbidden, it existed in concealed form (see substory below).

The sporting heroes of the sixties were generally in their teens or early twenties. Standards were so high that players rarely lasted long after their absolute physical peak was past. Sporting careers therefore tended to be shorter, and even more fiercely competitive.

While they were at the top, sportsmen were on T.V. and in newspapers all the time. A boxer like Cassius Clay, a footballer like George Best, was constantly followed, photographed and quoted—and had his private life investigated and reported.

The growing popularity of television helped to make sportsmen into national or even international idols. Inevitably, it popularised sports that televised well—above all football, firmly established as *the* international sport.

Sport and business became closely connected in the sixties. Rising costs made it hard to finance any but mass sports like football, and players often had money troubles. In motor racing, for example, few drivers could hope to win enough prize money to pay for themselves, their travel expenses, crews and cars.

Increasingly, big firms stepped in to stage events (horse races, chess tournaments, tennis and golf competitions), put up large prizes, or sponsored the competitors themselves. Naturally they hoped to benefit from the advertisement value of their activities. Here cosmetics and tyres are displayed on a car.

Financing of "amateurs" was less direct. Many U.S. athletes worked at colleges where they were allowed unlimited free time and first-class facilities. In other countries, sportsmen were given similar advantages while serving as army officers. And in all Communist countries they were effectively state-financed. So in practice even the Olympics were largely "professional" affairs.

▲ **"Riding the wild surf"** became a fabled pastime during the 1960s. Originally an import from the Hawaiian Islands, surfing caught the imagination of an entire generation. The Pacific Islands, California, South Africa and Australia were its leading centres, but films, pop songs and travelling "surf bums" spread enthusiasm for this exhilarating sport.

▲ **Politics in sport.** On the winners' stand at the 1968 Mexico City Olympics, two American Negroes give the clenched-fist salute. This declared their allegiance to "Black Power", and was intended to embarrass the U.S.— which it did.

◀ **Gymnastic display in East Germany.** Sporting achievements were useful as national propaganda. They also added to the prestige of the government in power— often sorely needed, as in East Germany, which received little international recognition.

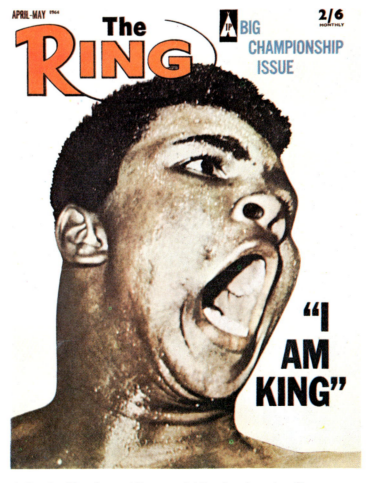

▲ **The bullfighter demonstrates his skill:** El Cordobes, most famous of post-war matadors, brings the bull in very close as it passes him. Unlike many national sports, bullfighting retained its popularity, though Spaniards were also football-crazy.

▲ **Cassius Clay,** the world heavyweight boxing champion. Clay was an entertaining personality who loved to show off and make up rhymes about his exploits. He changed his name to Muhammed Ali after being converted to the Black Muslim sect.

Europe United?

After centuries of conflict, the nations of western Europe had at last learned to work together.

Half of Europe was under Communist rule, and bound to Russia by military and economic ties. The western European states, shorn of their colonies, could only remain a force in the world by close collaboration. And so they set up a number of organisations, including a Council of Europe which met at Strasbourg.

But few governments were willing to hand over their powers to such bodies. Only six could agree to move quickly towards economic and political union. In 1958 "The Six" formed the E.E.C. (European Economic Community) or Common Market.

Economically, the E.E.C. was to be a free trade area—that is, tariffs (taxes on imported goods) were to be abolished between member-countries. And they would all levy the same tariffs on goods from outside the Market, behaving—at least commercially—as if the whole area was a single country.

The programme was evidently a success, for production and trade grew at a tremendous rate. Britain and other European states which had not joined the Market were spurred to form a rival free trade area, E.F.T.A., in 1960. But the pull of the Market was so strong that within a year Britain was trying to become a member.

Progress towards political unity was slower. France insisted on her right to veto majority decisions, and proposals for an elected "European" parliament came to nothing. By 1969 the Common Market seemed about to enlarge and to grow still more prosperous; but it was not certain it would become a real United States of Europe.

◀ **De Gaulle blocks British membership** of the Common Market. This cartoon comments on the British application of 1967, made by Harold Wilson's government; an earlier failure— under Macmillan—is marked further down the ladder. Most E.E.C. countries wanted Britain to join, but de Gaulle argued that she was too involved with the U.S.A. and the Commonwealth to make a "good European".

▲ **Europe's largest and busiest port:** Hamburg in Germany. The German "economic miracle" carried on steadily through the sixties, though de Gaulle's political flair made France seem more important for a time. The whole Common Market prospered, but Germany's exceptional strength was shown by the money crisis of 1969, which ended with the upward revaluation of German currency.

TWO TROUBLESPOTS

◀ **Greek democracy** was overthrown by a right-wing army coup in April 1967. Many people were imprisoned, and strict censorship was imposed. Later in the year King Constantine made an unsuccessful attempt to end military rule and fled to Italy. In the Russian cartoon, a Greek soldier is executing justice.

▼ **Northern Ireland** was dominated by a Protestant majority. In 1968 a civil rights movement was formed to win better treatment for the Catholic minority. Violence built up between the two groups, and though the British army was sent in to keep order, terrorism increased and even spread to England.

▲ **A Common Market "summit", 1969.** In the front row sit the national leaders: Rumor (Italy), Brandt (West Germany), Pompidou (France), de Jong (Holland), Eyskens (Belgium). Their most important decision was to hold talks with Britain, Ireland, Denmark and Norway, all of whom wished to join E.E.C. De Gaulle's fall had now made British membership a possibility.

▶ **The European idea** is the theme of these stamps issued by the Common Market "Six": Italy, Belgium, Holland, Luxembourg, France, and West Germany. In practice, however, there were still important conflicts of national interest. The other West European group was the E.F.T.A. "Seven": Britain, Sweden, Denmark, Norway, Switzerland, Austria and Portugal.

De Gaulle's France

Deeply divided, France turned to her wartime leader, General de Gaulle, in the hope that all Frenchmen would rally to him.

▲ **Prosperous young people of Paris.** De Gaulle's France shared in European affluence; Gaullism received much of the credit, though a good deal of the planning had been done under the less politically stable Fourth Republic. Eruption of student dissent in 1968 took the regime by surprise, but the police responded in force.

▼ **Grim riot police in Paris.** The student-worker "revolution" of May 1968 (page 52) showed up the weaknesses of the seventy-nine year-old de Gaulle's rule. Gaullists' won the next election by playing on fears of revolution, but confidence in de Gaulle himself was shaken. In the following year he was defeated in a referendum and resigned.

Weak, short-lived governments had failed to cope with France's problems—above all, with the long Algerian rebellion. In 1958, when the army and French population of Algeria refused to obey their own government, the legendary de Gaulle seemed the only man who might save the situation.

De Gaulle would only take over on his own terms. The constitution of his new Fifth Republic gave the president far wider powers—and of course the president was de Gaulle.

Many of his supporters had expected him to back the army's fight in Algeria. Instead, de Gaulle became convinced that independence was inevitable for Algeria and other French African states, and granted it in spite of all opposition.

De Gaulle's policy became firmly centred on Europe. He worked closely with West Germany, stopped the "un-European" British joining the E.E.C. (page 22), and withdrew from the U.S. dominated N.A.T.O. alliance. But he kept an exaggerated idea of French greatness, and insisted that French nuclear weapons be made and tested.

De Gaulle believed in strong government, but he was no dictator. Parliament continued to function, but he often appealed directly to the people by holding a referendum, in which everyone could vote to approve or reject a particular policy.

In 1969, defeated in such a referendum, the ageing de Gaulle resigned. But his system—and a strong, stable France—remained.

▶ **Cartoon of de Gaulle,** based on a painting of France's "Sun King", Louis XIV. The suggestion is that de Gaulle and his authoritarian rule belong in a museum. The figure in the lower left-hand corner is Georges Pompidou, who succeeded de Gaulle as president.

AU MUSÉE !..

CHARLES DE·GAULLE REGNANTE (1958.1965.19

...LE MONARQUE

The Six Day War

▼ **The surprise attack on June 5** ensured victory for Israel against her most powerful enemy, Egypt. The Egyptian airforce was destroyed on the ground when her airfields were bombed. Egypt's army was encircled and defeated in the Sinai desert. Jordan unwisely entered the war, only to be driven after bitter fighting from Jerusalem and the whole left bank of the River Jordan. In the last 24 hours of the war the Israelis stormed the Golan Heights, from which the Syrians had shelled Israeli settlements since 1948.

The Arabs had long been determined to wipe out Israel, the Jewish state in Palestine. Israel's swift, shattering victory of 1967 answered the threat, but brought peace no closer.

To Arabs, Israel was a land stolen from the Palestinians, a million of whom lived as refugees in camps near Israel's borders. Even after losing two wars (in 1948 and 1956), Arab states such as Egypt, Jordan and Syria continued to support Palestinian guerrilla attacks on Israel.

The great powers were involved too. Russia lent the Arabs great support, so gaining great influence in the Middle East. The United States, though less one-sided, gave Israel a good deal of help.

The 1967 crisis began when President Nasser of Egypt made several threatening moves. One was to close the Straits of Tiran to Israeli ships—an action Israel had warned would mean war. Then Nasser signed a treaty with his long-time enemy King Hussein of Jordan. Believing the Arabs were about to attack, Israel struck first.

Early on the morning of June 5, 1967 waves of Israeli planes flew under the Egyptian radar and smashed Egypt's planes and airfields. Israeli tanks plunged deep into Sinai and routed the Egyptian army. And Jordan and Syria were punished almost as severely before Israel accepted the U.N. order for a cease-fire.

This was Israel's third and most crushing victory over the Arabs. In six days the whole of Sinai, the west bank of the River Jordan and Syria's Golan Heights had fallen. Now, if the Arabs wanted their territory back, they would have to agree to a lasting peace with Israel. Meanwhile Israel's new borders—the Heights, the Jordan, the Suez Canal—were much easier to defend than her old ones.

But peace did not come, partly because of the Palestinians' opposition to compromise (see opposite). Israel made peace less likely by declaring she would never give back Jerusalem, the Holy City captured from Jordan. And in the meantime Israel had to organise occupied territories inhabited by a million hostile Arabs.

And so, instead of peace, the cycle of raids, reprisals and diplomacy carried on into the seventies.

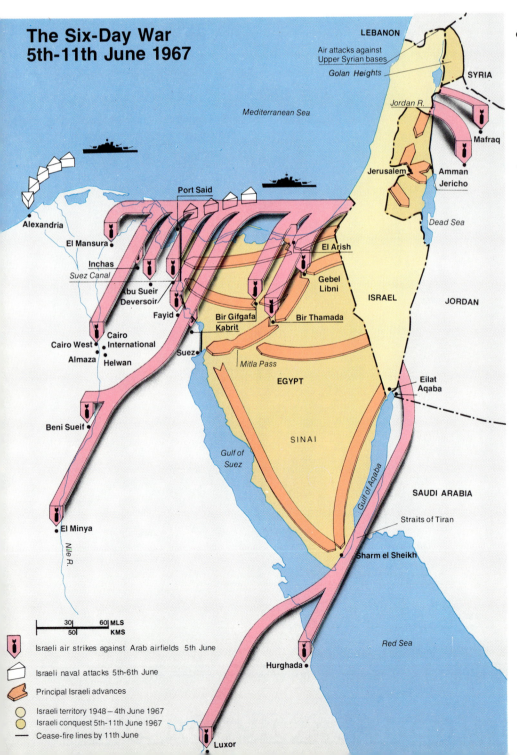

**The Six-Day War
5th-11th June 1967**

LEBANON

Air attacks against Upper Syrian bases

Golan Heights

SYRIA

Mediterranean Sea

Jordan R.

Mafraq

Port Said

Jerusalem

Amman
Jericho

Alexandria

El Mansura

Inchas

Suez Canal

El Arish

Dead Sea

Abu Sueir
Deversoir

Gebel
Libni

ISRAEL

JORDAN

Fayid

Bir Gifgafa
Kabrit

Bir Thamada

Cairo
International

Cairo West

Almaza

Helwan

Suez

Mitla Pass

Eilat
Aqaba

EGYPT

Beni Sueif

SINAI

Gulf of
Suez

Gulf of Aqaba

SAUDI ARABIA

Straits of Tiran

El Minya

Nile R.

Sharm el Sheikh

30   60 MLS
   50   KMS

Red Sea

Israeli air strikes against Arab airfields 5th June

Israeli naval attacks 5th-6th June

Principal Israeli advances

Israeli territory 1948 – 4th June 1967

Israeli conquest 5th-11th June 1967

Cease-fire lines by 11th June

Hurghada

Luxor

A New Force Emerges

The plight of the Palestinian refugees, homeless since 1948, had aroused the world's sympathy. In the sixties they emerged as a militant independent force, with political and guerrilla organisations bent on stopping any compromise settlement.

The Palestinians' attacks on Israel soon became terroristic (planting bombs and killing at random). Some groups began hijacking Israel's air liners and attacking her embassies on foreign soil; and in some countries the lives of Jewish citizens were threatened. When such terrorists were imprisoned, their comrades used hijacking and kidnapping tactics against the country concerned.

◀ **The Palestinian refugees** posed one of the most distressing human problems of the war.

▲ **An Egyptian tank blazes in the desert.** After the Israeli victory Sinai was littered with Russian-supplied tanks, smashed in the duel with Israel's armour—supplied by the U.S.A.

But skill and daring gave the Israelis their overwhelming success. Even as the Egyptians were being pushed back from the border areas, Israeli tanks outflanked them and raced to cut them off at Mitla Pass. Trapped, the Egyptians were pounded and starved into surrender.

Czechoslovakia Invaded

▲ **Alexander Dubcek** (pronounced Doob-check) was a Moscow-trained Communist. But as Czech leader his reforms outraged the Russians.

Czechoslovakia was the first Communist state to relax its restraints on the individual. Its invasion by Russia shocked the world and dashed liberal hopes in Eastern Europe.

Conditions in the Soviet bloc improved greatly in the fifties and sixties. Russia's East European "satellites" were allowed more independence, and there were no more bloody "purges" and mass spy trials. But if there was less terror, there was not much more freedom.

In Czechoslovakia pressure for change was so strong that, in January 1968, a new reforming leader took over: Alexander Dubcek.

Within three months life in Czechoslovakia was transformed. The people were given basic freedoms such as the right to travel abroad. Press and T.V. were freed from control, letting loose a torrent of criticism of past abuses. And an attempt was made to decentralise the flagging economy.

Dubcek was a sincere Communist who recognised the value of free discussion. But the Russians and their other allies feared that it might undermine their power and even bring down the whole Communist system. Though Dubcek assured them that Czechoslovakia would remain faithful to the Warsaw Pact (the Communist alliance), the Russians decided to make sure.

The operation was swift and efficient. Late at night, Warsaw Pact tanks rumbled across the Czech border; and others were soon being flown into Prague airport. By early morning of August 21, 1968, the main Czech cities had been occupied.

The Russians claimed that there was a Western plot against which they had to protect the Czechs. They also tried to make out that the Czechs had asked them to come; but the Czech people were so united against them that they had to drop the story.

For a time Dubcek and his followers were even left in office, though they had to give up more and more of their reforms under "comradely" pressure from the army of occupation. And at last Dubcek himself was removed: the Czech experiment had come to an end.

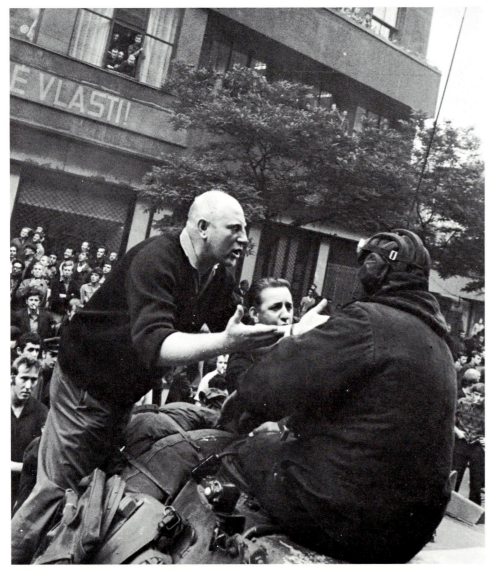

◀ **Czechs harangue a Russian tank commander.** The Russian troops obeyed orders, but even they must have wondered about Russia's obviously unpopular occupation of a fellow Communist country. Communist Parties in the West opposed it, but critics in Russia were soon silenced.

▶ **Czech resistance was non-violent.** The Czechs clearly had no chance against the Russians, so Dubcek's government ordered them not to fight. Instead, they showed their feelings by demonstrations and acts of defiance, like these mourners for a boy killed in the invasion.

The Third World

In the fifties, the Cold War seemed to split the world in two. The sixties brought many new independent nations into the U.N. – a "Third World" with quite different problems of its own.

▼ **Poverty and technical backwardness** went together in places like this Nigerian village. Disease and famine threatened millions even in "good" years. Some economists argued that Third World countries should not try to build huge, expensive Western-style factories. They favoured a different, smaller-scale technology which would make use of the abundant manpower.

Most Western and Communist countries had advanced economies and high standards of living. Generally speaking, they had become wealthy by developing industries. The Third World—most of Asia, Africa and South America—consisted of poor, economically "underdeveloped" states producing foodstuffs or raw materials.

It had always been assumed that the Third World would gradually catch up and become industrialised. But by the sixties this was clearly not happening. West and East were producing more and more abundantly; elsewhere, progress was painfully slow, so that the gap between "worlds" actually grew wider.

Some countries even became poorer, for the Third World's population was rising incredibly fast—which meant there was often less food and resources to go around. The "population explosion" was largely caused by Western medicine, which had wiped out most killer diseases (especially of mothers and children). Unfortunately there was no equally effective way of increasing production to match.

Overpopulation brought unemployment, malnutrition, overcrowding (often in slums and tin-shack "shanty towns"), the overworking of exhausted soils, and many other ills. And poor, overpopulated countries could not educate or train their peoples, so that industrial development became still harder to achieve.

The wealthier nations did try to help with food, credit, materials and technical advice—often to win the Third World's political friendship. Some impressive projects were finished, such as Egypt's Russian-built Aswan Dam and the Chinese-built Tanzam railway in Africa. The U.N. administered aid schemes and organized relief for countries hit by flood or famine. Yet at the end of the sixties, the problem was as great as ever.

▶ **Nationalism** was a powerful force in the Third World. As this poster shows, there was also a feeling of kinship among Third World countries. Though not necessarily pro-Russian or Chinese, most of them were suspicious of the West, often accusing the U.S. and ex-colonial powers of trying to control them indirectly ("neo-colonialism").

坚决支持亚洲非洲拉丁

Vietnam

Communist activity in South Vietnam led the United States to intervene in force. Unable to win victory, the U.S. suffered a serious blow to her prestige and morale.

In 1954 Vietnam was divided into a Communist North and a non-Communist South. Communist guerrillas, the Viet Cong, became active in the South from 1960; they received aid from North Vietnam, while the United States supplied South Vietnam with equipment and U.S. advisers.

The successes of the Viet Cong, now helped by regular army units from North Vietnam, made the U.S. take a tougher line. The U.S. armed forces were sent to Vietnam, theoretically still as "advisers" but in reality to fight. And beginning in 1964, U.S. President Johnson ordered heavy bombing of the North.

Over half a million American soldiers eventually fought in Vietnam, but they could never pin down and destroy the Viet Cong. And though North Vietnam was bombed mercilessly, the Communists would not weaken.

The cost of the war in money and lives worried Americans more and more. Then, in January 1968, the Communists launched the great Tet offensive. It was beaten off, but it showed a U.S. victory was not in sight.

The last straw was the news that another 200,000 troops were needed. Johnson called off the bombing of the North and agreed to peace talks. And in 1969 a new president, Nixon, announced that the army of South Vietnam would take over the whole defence of the country. The U.S. would give massive assistance but all U.S. troops would be withdrawn—a triumph for the Communist camp. The war itself dragged on relentlessly into the seventies.

▼ **Map of the war,** showing how North Vietnam managed to send men and munitions to the South—through neutral Laos and Cambodia.

The Vietnam War since 1964
Key:
- Demilitarized Zone
- American base now abandoned
- **Ho Chi Minh Trail** Communist Infiltration Routes
- **Sihanouk Trail**
- Railway
- Major areas of fighting

▼ **Buddhist priests,** representative of Vietnam's ancient culture, but also politically militant in the complicated politics of the South.

▲ **The Viet Cong guerrillas** travelled light and fast, and hit very hard. Even America's earth-scorching napalm bombs failed to flush them out of the jungle.

◀ **U.S. technology** was the most advanced in the world, but failed to bring victory. And U.S. installations like this blazing dump were never safe from guerrilla attack.

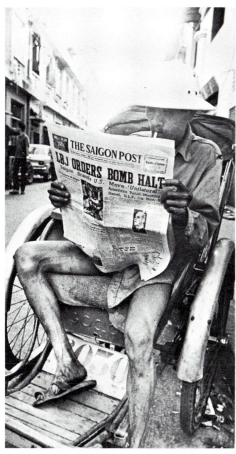

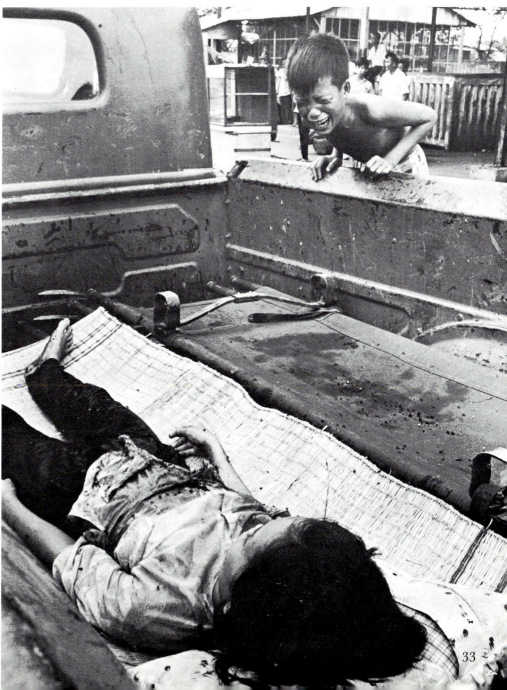

▲ **Newspaper and T.V. reporting** deeply influenced the course of the war. Detailed descriptions and on-the-spot pictures made people all over the world feel involved. In particular they aroused anti-American feelings by showing the mighty U.S.A. battering tiny North Vietnam day after day—and failing to make her submit. Hostile world opinion, and opposition inside the U.S., speeded the U.S. decisions to halt the bombing and to withdraw.

▶ **A boy cries over his dead sister,** the victim of a U.S. flyer's mistake. This was only one of many ways in which the innocent suffered.

Entertainment and Leisure

Holidays

A new major industry: tourism. Millions of people went abroad for their holidays, often for the first time. Many companies prospered by taking care of the timid tourist who was handicapped by not knowing the local language and by limited time and money. The "package holiday" did away with all these problems. Transport, hotel bookings, meals and "optional extras" were arranged for the holidaymaker, and guides and couriers helped him at every stage. Package holidays were surprisingly cheap, since the organising company could get discounts on "block" (mass) bookings.

Fun and fantasy on holiday. American women in Hawaii, dressed "native-style".

Western affluence meant more money, and more leisure time and goods to spend it on. People found much of their entertainment at home – but also travelled further for it than ever before.

Television was established as regular evening entertainment for most families, and the development of colour pictures made it still more attractive. In these circumstances it was bound to influence people strongly, so that there were many debates about the quality and value of programmes. In Great Britain and the U.S., advertisers, who controlled commercial channels, were often blamed for poor taste; some people suggested that T.V. made people too passive—too ready to watch rather than follow hobbies or talk, and even unwilling to go out.

The cinema—the mass art of the forties—was still quite popular but no longer a rival to T.V. The most successful films were generally "epics" or musicals—lavishly set, star-studded, and lasting several hours.

Music played a larger part in many people's lives, and this too could be brought more effectively into the home. Tape recorders, and hi-fi and stereo record players improved in quality and became relatively cheap; and so did records.

On the other hand, people travelled more than ever before. Owning a car made short trips popular on weekends and public holidays, and many took their cars with them on holidays abroad.

Millions preferred the trouble-free escape provided by organized "package tours". But young people tended to be more adventurous and ready to rough it: they often travelled thousands of miles on little money, often as far as India and Nepal.

Flying became much cheaper. When air travel became common, planes could be specially chartered at cut prices. The sixties were the age of mass travel and people often remarked that the globe had "shrunk".

Televisions and private motor vehicles by selected countries, 1967

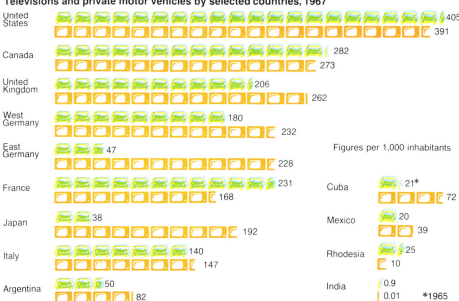

Figures per 1,000 inhabitants

Country	Motor vehicles	Televisions
United States	405	391
Canada	282	273
United Kingdom	206	262
West Germany	180	232
East Germany	47	228
France	231	168
Japan	38	192
Italy	140	147
Argentina	50	82
Cuba	21*	72
Mexico	20	39
Rhodesia	25	10
India	0.9	0.01

*1965

▲ **Television sets and motor cars** are the most sought-after mass-produced luxuries; "affluent societies" are those in which such goods have reached the mass of the people. As we might expect, the table shows the industrial countries far in the lead. With 405 cars for every 1,000 people, the overwhelming majority of U.S. families obviously ran a car. "Two-car families" were quite common, and many Americans bought a new model each year. By contrast, in India only the rich could afford a car or T.V. even once in a lifetime.

▶ **Bonnie and Clyde,** based on the exploits of real bankrobbers in the twenties, started a fashion for "gangster" clothes.

▼ **Cleopatra** starred Richard Burton and Elizabeth Taylor. This film was a typical "blockbuster", costing (and making) millions of dollars.

▼ **Bowling** had been a popular entertainment in the U.S. for many years. It never really caught on in Europe, though in Britain it was briefly fashionable in the early sixties.

America in Turmoil

▲ **Lyndon B. Johnson.** The Vietnam issue ruined his presidential career.

The U.S.A., the most powerful nation on Earth, dominated the post-war period – until American confidence was shattered by a disastrous war and a wave of violence and protest at home.

In 1963 Lyndon Johnson became U.S. President, and launched a great programme of social welfare. In spite of American prosperity there were still poor people who needed help, jobs or medical care; and negroes and other minorities suffered from prejudice and lack of opportunity. Johnson's reforms were popular, and he was triumphantly re-elected in 1964.

But there were already signs of unrest in the U.S. Almost every year violent riots raged in the black quarters of Chicago, Detroit and other big cities. Lives were lost and many buildings looted or burned down.

The riots awakened America to the frustration of black people in the Northern cities. In the South there had long been open injustice, but Northern minorities too suffered from prejudice and poverty, living in slums in the middle of the "affluent society".

The Vietnam war (page 32) was even more demoralising. U.S. failures, the loss of American lives, and doubts about the justice of the war led to protests that swelled into a national movement. Students, intellectuals, radicals and citizens of all classes and types took part. Feelings ran so high that many young men publicly burned their draft cards (calling them to the army) or went abroad to avoid serving.

Pressure on Johnson grew so great that he decided not to stand for re-election. The next president was the much more conservative Richard Nixon. But student radicalism went on spreading, and there was trouble at many universities. At one, Kent State in Ohio, four students were shot dead by National Guardsmen in May, 1970.

In these years America seemed on the verge of chaos. Many young people "dropped out"—rejected conventional careers and values. Violence exploded again in the assassinations of Martin Luther King and Senator Robert Kennedy. Many Blacks turned from non-violence to belief in revolution. And above all the war continued to divide America into two camps.

◀ **Martin Luther King** lies in state. King, a Baptist minister, led a series of non-violent protests against injustice towards Negroes in the Southern states (separate and inferior housing, schools, transport; denial of legal voting rights). But by the mid-sixties many Negroes felt that peaceful methods were not working. King's assassination in 1968 was another victory for violence, sparking off race riots in over a hundred cities.

◄ **Demonstration against Richard Nixon, 1968.** The banner slogan claims that Nixon's four-year term of office will mean four years of war in Vietnam. Nixon was the ''law and order'' candidate, and his election showed that most Americans were against radicalism and violence.

But the U.S.A. began to settle down only in the seventies, after Nixon had withdrawn troops from Vietnam. Without anti-war feeling to unite and popularise it, the ''New Left'' lost much of its following and student radicalism declined.

▼ **The Black Panthers** were one of the revolutionary groups thrown up in the sixties by the apparent failure of civil rights laws and peaceful protest. The Panthers' aggressive ''Black Power'' slogans represented one reaction to this. Another was the Black Muslim movement, combining Muslim religion— significantly, a non-Western belief—with a programme of dividing the U.S. between blacks and whites.

Even Negroes who did not take up such extreme positions tended to reject white values and emphasise their black and African heritage.

Transport and Travel

More travel and more trade kept transport booming through the sixties, and encouraged new technical advances.

▲ **The hovercraft** was an ingenious British invention, designed to travel over land and water on a cushion of air. The first cross-Channel service started in 1968.

With increasing affluence, private motoring became almost universal in the West. The prestige of car ownership encouraged people to drive to work when it was not necessary, adding to the already serious traffic problems. Clear, long-distance roads—motorways (U.K.), freeways (U.S.), autobahns (Germany), autostrada (Italy)—spread out over the West in an attempt to cope.

Air travel also boomed. Established airlines expanded their business and many companies sprang up to offer planes for hire. These chartered flights became enormously popular, particularly with travel agents selling package holidays (page 34).

Larger and faster aircraft were developed. Jet planes came into wide use as transports, and supersonic transports were put into production. By 1970 the "Jumbo jet"—a wide-bodied giant that could carry up to 500 passengers—seemed to promise cheaper flights.

Travel by sea had now become much too expensive for cruises, and too slow to compete with aeroplanes. On the other hand, trade by sea was more important than ever, for it was the most economical way of transporting bulky goods like oil, coal and iron. Many giant ships were built for such specialised tasks.

If the day of the giant liners was passing, smaller boats were actually owned by many people—motor boats that could be towed to the nearest coast, or yachts that could be moored in one of the new marinas being built in many places. Here too affluence imposed new patterns of development.

◀ **Japanese monorail train,** the first brought into service (1964). The mono (single) rail meant that there were no trains crossing the track and no stops: the train could travel at 100 miles an hour or more, carrying passengers rapidly from one big population centre to another. Even more ambitious plans were made for future high speed trains.

▲ **Concorde** was a jet transport developed and built jointly by Britain and France. It was one of the new class of supersonic transports (supersonic means faster than sound). It could fly at well over 1,000 miles an hour, but like other supersonic craft it raised objections on social grounds, due to general noisiness and the deafening ''sonic boom'' it produced when breaking the sound barrier. Concorde began regular service in 1976.

▶ **Road networks** became increasingly complex. This one brings half a dozen roads out on to a bridge over the River Rhine in Germany. Like the one outside Birmingham it could well be called ''spaghetti junction''. Inside towns, where the chaos was worst, flyovers and other devices brought some relief. But drastic proposals for new road systems were generally resisted, since they involved destroying badly needed houses and disrupting the life of old-established areas.

▶ **''Why can't you pick a space your own size?''** roars the angry motorist. The cartoon points up the desperate lack of parking space in towns. The offending car, incidentally, is an English Mini—hugely popular for, among other things, the compactness that enabled it to fit into any available parking space.

▼ **Italian sports cars** came to the fore in this decade. Luxury designs like the Ferrari, the Maserati and this Lamborghini were envied status symbols. Ferruccio Lamborghini makes tractors, but he began producing cars in 1963. Late sixties' prototypes reached speeds around 190 mph.

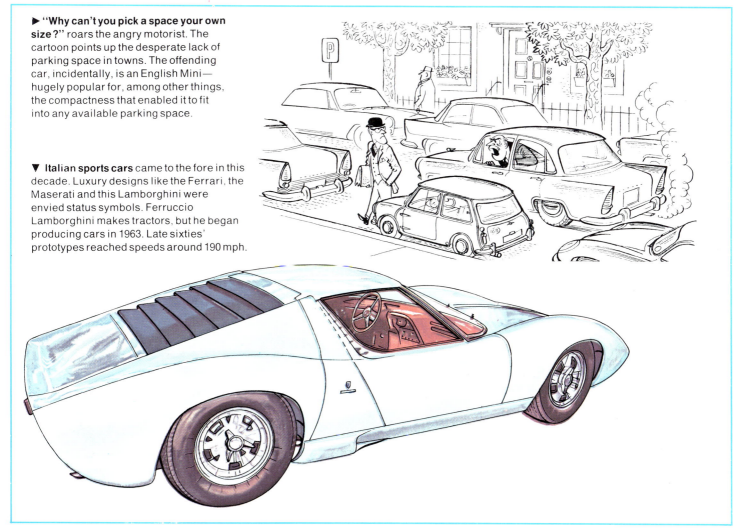

Science and Progress

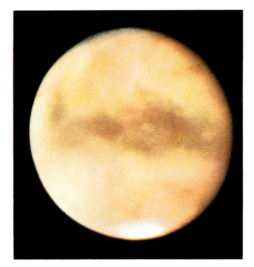

The rapid progress of science and technology gave rise to wild hopes and fears. Was man heading for Utopia – or for doom?

Man's knowledge of the solar system, and even of other galaxies, grew rapidly. On Earth, discoveries in Africa revealed that man was more than two million years older than previously believed. And the chemical make-up of life itself began to be understood.

Yet science uncovered as many mysteries as it solved. On the "sub-atomic" level (concerned with the tiniest particles), cause and effect seemed not to work; and in the strange world of deep space, ordinary ideas of mass, density and even time lost most of their relevance.

But in the practical field of technology, scientific research produced solid results. Man went out into space (page 42), and also down to the deepest part of the ocean bed in a "bathyscaphe". He could communicate across the ocean via artificial satellites, and travel by supersonic jets and high-speed trains.

Society itself was being transformed by computers, electronic machines designed to store and sort information, "think" and "calculate" at fantastic speeds. This was one of many forms of automation—the replacement of human work by machines, whether for dish-washing or predicting weather.

Some people saw computers and automation as keys to Utopia, an ideal society of abundant goods and leisure. Others feared that individuals would become powerless in a machine-run world. And there were still others who pointed out that technology was not improving but ruining life and the whole planet (page 44).

The problem came back to man himself. Every advance in his power over nature gave him new weapons with which to make the good life or destroy himself. At the end of the sixties it was still not clear which course he would choose.

The gigantic and the miniscule, revealed by science. Above : the planets Mars, Jupiter and Saturn (with the rings). Unmanned spacecraft reached Mars in the sixties. Right : part of the human liver. Green dye has been injected into it to show up the tiny veins.

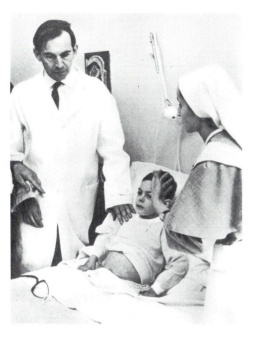

▲ **Dr Christiaan Barnard** with a heart patient. In 1967 Barnard, a South African, performed the most dramatic operation of the sixties: the first heart transplant. This involved removing the heart from one body (of a person who had just died) and planting it in the body of a person about to die of heart failure. One heart transplant enabled the patient to live a further 19 months. However, the value of the operation remained controversial.

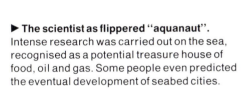

► **The scientist as flippered "aquanaut".** Intense research was carried out on the sea, recognised as a potential treasure house of food, oil and gas. Some people even predicted the eventual development of seabed cities.

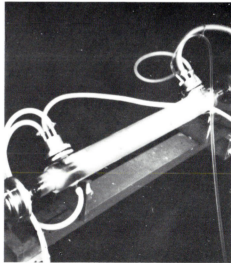

▲ **The maser,** a device for producing microwaves, was invented in the fifties; from it was developed the laser. This gave out an intense beam of light or, more dramatically, hot, cutting infra-red rays used (e.g.) in surgery.

◄ **Computers** became common in the West during the sixties, processing and controlling many large-scale operations. This one, on the liner Queen Elizabeth II, enabled one man to check the whole ship for safety faults.

Space Exploration

The Space Age began in 1957, when Russia sent up Sputnik 1, which went into orbit round the Earth. But few could foresee the giant strides of the sixties.

The first man in space was the Russian astronaut Yuri Gagarin. His 1961 flight in Vostok 1 proved once and for all that man could survive in space. By a terrible irony, Gagarin was to be killed in a plane crash in 1968.

▼ **Telstar** was a communications satellite. With equipment like this "antenna", signals could be sent across the Atlantic via Telstar.

The Earth was soon being circled by hundreds of man-made satellites, equipped with scientific instruments. Some recorded the patterns of cloud and wind, making weather forecasting more reliable. Some sent back information about the Earth itself, using infra-red and other photographic techniques. Many were "spies in the sky", made to record information of military value.

Other spacecraft went out into the solar system and sent back information and pictures. In 1959 Russia's Luna 3 had photographed the hidden side of the Moon, and in the sixties American and Russian craft reached Mars and Venus.

But public interest was concentrated on the human side of the story: the possibility of manned space flight. In this the Russians led all through the early sixties. They put the first man into space (Gagarin, 1961), and later the first woman. In 1965 a Russian astronaut took the first "space walk", which made it possible to do repairs and other jobs outside the craft. And an unmanned Russian spacecraft even made the first "soft" landing on the Moon, sending back pictures that proved the surface was firm enough to land on.

A great American effort to catch up with Russia in the "space race" was started by President Kennedy in 1961. The aim was to put a man on the Moon by 1970. By the late sixties the Russians seemed to have lost interest in this (probably because of the enormous expense), and the U.S. went steadily forward on her own.

On July 20, 1969 the expense and effort were rewarded. After long preparation and several rehearsals, the first man stepped out on to the Moon.

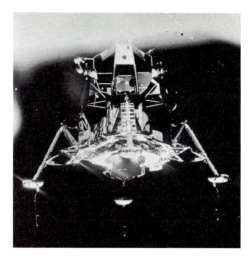

Far left: Lift-off! The Apollo 11 mission begins its historic journey from Cape Kennedy to the Moon.

Top left: Two minutes forty seconds later. The first stage of the rocket about to be cast off.

Left: The command-service module, with astronaut Collins inside, sixty miles above the Moon's surface.

Above: The lunar module, about to carry Armstrong and Aldrin down to the Sea of Tranquillity.

Below left: The first man to walk on the Moon, astronaut Neil Armstrong, salutes the U.S. flag.

Below: End of a mission. Splashdown in the Pacific—and, for the astronauts, a cautious spraying with disinfectant.

The Moon Landing

Apollo 11 was launched from Cape Kennedy, Florida, on 16th July 1969. On the 20th, two of its crew, Neil Armstrong and Edwin Aldrin, actually landed on the Moon's surface. Armstrong stepped out of the lunar module and so became the first man to set foot on the Moon.

Apollo 11 was not a single powerful rocket, of the sort predicted by most science fiction writers. It was a complicated machine that shed used-up parts in the course of the journey. This process started with the launching vehicle, Saturn 5, which was discarded in three stages, as it first put Apollo 11 into orbit round the Earth and then blasted it into space.

Another tremendously impressive feature of the journey was the separation and re-linking ("docking") of two parts of the craft. This manoeuvre had to be done twice with the command-service module and the lunar module. The actual descent on to the Moon's sur-

face was made by the lunar module; the command-service module, carrying Collins, remained in orbit round the Moon.

For the return trip the lunar module brought Armstrong and Aldrin back to the command-service module and was then discarded. Before entering the Earth's atmosphere, the service module was cast off too. The command module —a cone only a fraction the size of the original craft—splashed down safely in the Pacific.

The Cost of Affluence

Man has used technology to master the Earth. Now he is in danger of ruining it – and his own future.

People had long known the dangers of the radioactive "fallout" produced by nuclear explosions. In the sixties they realised with a shock that technology often produced an equally disastrous effect on nature.

The problem of pollution—the poisoning of earth, air and water—received most attention. Mass production created huge quantities of industrial waste. Pumped into rivers or dispersed as fumes, it could kill crops, birds and fish, and harm humans. Factory machines were dangerous—and so were millions of cars that pumped carbon monoxide gas from their exhausts.

Even ordinary rubbish was vast in quantity: used goods, wrappers, cans, papers and magazines. At the same time, the world's resources were being used up at breakneck speed. Some, like forests, could not be replaced fast enough; others, like copper and oil, could not be replaced at all.

The general rise in population kept the Third World poor (page 30). It also made city life everywhere less pleasant. There were housing shortages, overcrowding and bad sanitation in poorer areas. Many cities were now so big that they no longer worked properly: centres became traffic choked, communications and services declined. And the loneliness of city life was often blamed for high rates of mental illness.

Many solutions were proposed for all these problems, from birth control to recycling (re-use of "used-up" materials). Some experts believed that economic growth must be slowed down; others argued that technology would solve the problems it had created. The most hopeful signs in the sixties were the concern these issues aroused and the growing sense of public responsibility for the quality of life.

▲ **The excitement of city life** is the subject of this painting by the British artist Eduardo Paolozzi. It emphasizes the colourful, dynamic side of motors, electronic machinery, etc. But noise, crowds, fumes and traffic jams became problems of increasing concern in the sixties.

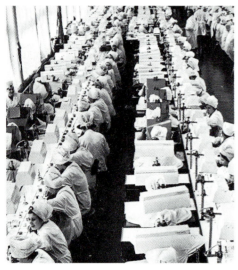

▲ **Lack of job satisfaction** is a problem in modern factories and offices, where workers often spend all day performing a single task, such as pulling a lever. Though frequently highly paid, these jobs can be monotonous, and give the worker no sense of achievement.

Town planning was recognized as important when it became clear that unplanned big cities were falling into chaos. Planners had to make sure that transport and communications worked efficiently, that low-cost housing prevented the growth of slums, and that the whole system would not seize up as population grew.

Population pressure was usually met by "high-rise" housing—tall blocks of flats which made it possible for a number of people to occupy a very small ground area. In practice, however, this often led to loneliness and the growth of crime.

The most daring experiment was Brasilia (above), an elegant new capital city built deep in Brazil's interior to an architect's careful designs. But even here, the growth of a slum shanty town on the outskirts of the city showed that artistic concepts of spaciousness and utility did not always meet the requirements of planning.

▲ **Polluted beaches:** soldiers with protective masks spray detergent on an oily Cornish beach.

◀ **Air pollution:** Scunthorpe ironworks, one source of industrial pollution. ''Smokeless zones'' in residential areas helped, but there was plenty of dirt from cars and furnaces.

▼ **Science and technology** can help control the environment—for example, by infra-red photographs taken from spacecraft. In this one of the Gulf of Mexico, diseased trees show up as blue, healthy ones as red.

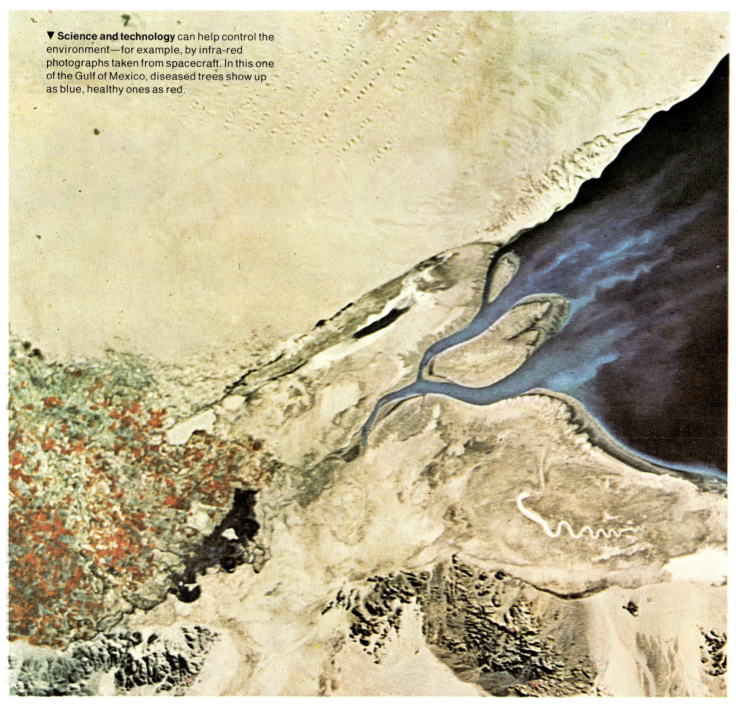

The Arts

Artistic experiment was bolder than ever in the sixties. The accepted definitions of art were questioned or even ignored.

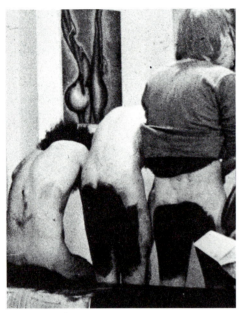

▲ **"Bottom Printing"**, one of many jokes at the expense of "serious" art. But equally serious claims were often made for the artistic importance of this kind of activity.

The main new visual style was Pop Art. This took its subjects from modern city life, and especially the "media"—films and magazines, T.V. serials, advertisements and comics. Usually Pop artists showed popular images in a different framework or material—the U.S. flag as a painting on canvas, Coca-Cola tins cast in bronze.

Modern technology could be harnessed to serve art. Machines produced brilliant, ever-changing electronic patterns. Sculptures became "kinetic"— or moveable—instead of remaining still. And electronic sounds were widely used in place of traditional instruments for musical compositions.

Many experiments challenged accepted ideas about art. There were cartoons made up into full-scale paintings, "music" consisting of silence, and "happenings" in which a frantic, semi-spontaneous action seemed more important than the final result. This kind of thing had been seen before in the mocking "anti-art" of the twenties (Dada, Surrealism) but was now presented as serious art.

In the theatre, realism was challenged by the idea of drama as ritual, seen in the plays of the French writer Jean Genet and the German Peter Weiss (*Marat/Sade*). In the novel, experiment, fantasy and science fiction became more popular.

Among other interesting trends of the sixties were performances and poetry readings in which audiences could take an active part, cheaply made experimental films, and colourful poster art.

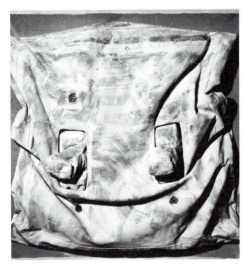

▲ **"Wall switches"**. Pop artist Claes Oldenburg specialised in making very large versions of ordinary things (hamburgers, drums, etc.) with materials that completely changed the impact they made. Here a surprise effect has been achieved by making a soft, sagging version of a hard, straight-edged object.

▶ **"Whaam!"** This painting—a copy of a frame from a comic—is typical of U.S. artist Roy Liechtenstein's work. Most Pop artists were straightforwardly fascinated by mass products of the Western—above all American— way of life. Enjoyment, rather than satire or comment, was characteristic of Pop.

▲ **Allen Ginsberg,** one of the "beat generation" of the fifties—drop-out writers who, in a sense, pioneered the "underground". Ginsberg's powerful, chant-like poetry, and his enthusiasm for peace, sex and Buddhism, made him a hero to the generation of the sixties.

▲ **Russian poet and rebel Yevgeni Yevtushenko.** In Russia the writer was traditionally involved in politics and questions of conscience. Yevtushenko was one of the leaders of the generation after Stalin, active in arguing for greater freedom, and in and out of trouble with the ruling Communist Party. Poetry readings were tremendously popular throughout Russia.

By the mid-sixties the authorities were again trying to control writers more strictly. Those whose style or viewpoint was "wrong" were not allowed to publish; but many books became known by being passed from hand to hand in typed copies. Russia's leading novelist, Alexander Solzhenitsyn, was published openly only outside the Communist bloc.

▲ **The novelist Norman Mailer,** a controversial figure who began in literature with a best seller about the U.S. army in World War Two. By the sixties he was a political and sexual radical, given to eccentric gestures. Much of his recent work has been a kind of personalised reporting rather than traditional fiction.

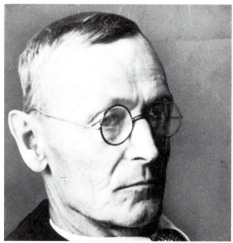

▲ **Hermann Hesse** was a German writer who died in 1962. Among young people, Hesse novels such as *Steppenwolf* and *Siddharta* became a cult. They are written in a poetic style and deal with the search for life's meaning. Eastern religion and the need for a "journey to the East" play a great part in Hesse's thinking.

The End of the Cold War?

▲ **Mao "encourages" Khrushchev** to be tough with Kennedy in this cartoon. In fact the frayed Communist alliance reached a crisis point over this issue.

▼ **An H-bomb** is cheered by Chinese workers waving the little red book, in this faked propaganda picture.

In the fifties, world war seemed possible at any time. In the sixties, relations between the great powers gradually improved.

With crises over U.S. spy planes, Berlin (page 6) and Cuba (page 4), the Cold War reached a climax in the early sixties. But in fact the Berlin Wall stabilised the situation in Europe, and the Cuban missile crisis convinced the Russians that the U.S. would take a tough line in the face of direct threats or intimidation.

After this, attitudes on both sides grew less aggressive. Led by Kennedy, the U.S. gave up some of her crusading anti-Communism. Russia became more cautious and conservative, probably because she was now a recognised great power with a rising standard of living—in other words, with everything to lose by risking war.

Both superpowers realised that all-out nuclear war would ruin them and perhaps destroy the world. But certain peace could come only if they agreed to reduce their huge arsenals of arms and missiles—a move they still distrusted each other too much to make.

The most definite advance was an agreement not to test nuclear bombs in the Earth's atmosphere. The propaganda war between East and West went on, and both manoeuvred to win new friends and allies. Yet there had been a real change, shown in the way each side avoided a showdown over issues like Vietnam (page 32) and Czechoslovakia (page 28).

By the seventies, Russia and the U.S. were ready to co-operate on space projects. World war, though still possible, now seemed a little less likely than before.

▲ **"Shall we resume testing human beings?"**
Here the bombs seem to control the politicians, not vice versa. The U.S., Russia and Britain signed a test ban, but some countries without stockpiles were less enthusiastic. China and France went on testing, and there were fears that still more would join the "nuclear club".

▲ **Kennedy and Khrushchev meet** in Vienna, 1961. Despite the handshakes, the Cold War seemed as threatening as ever, with a continuing crisis over Berlin and mounting tension over Cuba. But though Khrushchev's style of speech was aggressive, he had no desire to plunge the world into a nuclear war. He toned down the Communist belief that war between East and West was inevitable; instead, he declared, Communism would win in the course of "peaceful coexistence" between the great powers.

▶ **The Russian-Chinese split** broke the unity of the Communist world. It became public in 1960, when China supported Albania's anti-Soviet statements at the Moscow Conference. Russia withdrew all aid and advisers from China. By the late sixties relations were so bad that there were shooting incidents on the frontiers and disputes over territory. Here Russian and Chinese frontier guards argue a point in the Chenpao Island area. Russian fear of China made her even less aggressive towards the West.

◀ **U.S. president Nixon meets Chairman Mao, 1972.** In the sixties China was largely cut off from the outside world, and in a dangerous mood. Understandably, she saw the U.S. as her chief enemy. The U.S. refused to recognise Mao's government, protected the Communists' Chinese enemies on Taiwan, and kept China out of the United Nations. In the seventies U.S. policies would change: China would be admitted to the U.N., and Nixon would pay a visit to China.

The Permissive Society

In the sixties, many established Western values were crumbling. A "permissive society" evolved in which authority no longer tried to control some vital areas of private life.

In the sixties, many established Western values were challenged. Orthodox religion lost much of its influence, and many vital areas of life were no longer controlled by authority. The most important area was sex. Traditional teaching in the West represented sex before or outside marriage as sinful—though this was often ignored in practice. Now public attitudes changed. Discussion of sex became freer, and young people acquired a greater degree of responsibility in the conduct of their own lives. In many countries, "deviations" such as homosexuality were no longer criminal offenses, punishable by imprisonment.

Newspapers, films and other media made much of this, often exploiting sensational sex interest to boost sales.

There were many censorship battles, but generally speaking books, plays, films and television showed sex more and more openly.

This and other breaks with tradition caused fierce arguments. No doubt an individual should be free to please—or even harm—himself. But what about the social effects of, say, easier divorce? Was drug-taking a private or a public matter? Was it possible to distinguish between serious and "exploitative" descriptions of sex or violence? And did the young and immature need special protection?

Similar debates raged over subjects like "the Pill"—a new contraceptive for women—the abortion and divorce laws, and even over the savage, often insulting, satire then in fashion.

▲ **Eastern cults** became popular, especially among young people. Emphasis on mystical experience and non-violence fitted in with experiments with drugs and the "peace and love" mood stemming from the hippies. Here Maharishi Mahesh Yogi, teacher of Transcendental Meditation, is seen with film star Mia Farrow. For a time the Beatles were also his followers.

▶ **"Rebellion in the Church!"** symbolised by a "nun" baring a picture of the revolutionary Che Guevara. Catholics were notable for obedience to religious authority, so such rebellion was an impressive sign of the times.

This saucy magazine cover is typical of the "satire revolution" of the sixties, which hit out cheerfully in all directions.

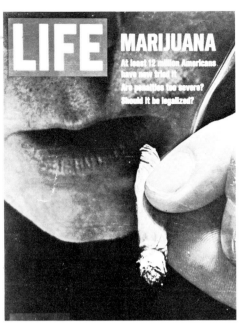

LIFE MARIJUANA

At least 12 million Americans have now tried it. Are penalties too severe? Should it be legalized?

◀ **The argument over marijuana,** a drug usually smoked like a cigarette, summarised by *Life*.

▼ **Books about sex** multiplied, despite fears that their influence might be "corrupting".

DER SPIEGEL

Papst Paul VI:

Nein zur Pille

51

▲ **"No" to the Pill.** The Catholic Church banned artificial birth control. To many Catholics this made little sense in an overpopulated world, but Paul VI rejected proposed changes.

▲ **James Bond** was a fictional character, taken over from Ian Fleming's popular novels into even more popular films (this one is *From Russia With Love*). Bond was a secret agent who killed ruthlessly—and with sadistic enjoyment—between sexual adventures. "Romance" and patriotism played no part in these stories, which were part of a great fashion for spy/agent films—many of them even more cynical about national loyalties.

With few exceptions, such films were not aiming for greater honesty but sensational impact. Though apparently realistic, they tended to glamorise violence and to make heroes of violent people (e.g. Bonnie and Clyde).

Protest!

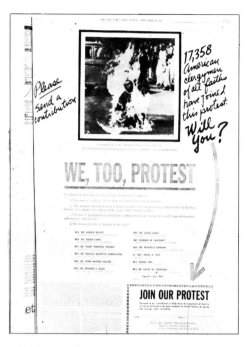

The affluence and freedom of the West seemed to make revolution impossible. But in the sixties there was a fresh wave of unrest, and a revolutionary "New Left" emerged.

The Communist Party had been the main revolutionary party down to the fifties, though outside France and Italy it had only a small following. The grey, authoritarian Communism of the party's model—Soviet Russia—made little appeal to prosperous, relatively free societies.

The "New Left" describes various groups formed in the sixties. Most of them aimed for some form of socialism or communism in which workers really controlled government and industry. They rejected traditional party politics, arguing that all the parties were basically conservative. Instead, they believed in direct action—in demonstrating, striking, occupying factories and universities.

The New Left made little headway until the late sixties, when opposition to U.S. action in Vietnam broke out into mass protests in many countries. New Leftists—often students—were prominent in these "demos", and the U.S.

itself was swept by student radicalism.

Elsewhere, the movement reached a peak in the 1968 "student revolution" (see opposite). By the early seventies it seemed to have died away, leaving the New Left again a small minority in Western universities.

▲ **Protest against the Vietnam war** involved many people who were not really "political", like the clergymen mentioned on this document. But the energy of the New Leftists, and the publicity they received, made them seem stronger than they actually were.

The photo on the document shows another form of protest—a Vietnamese monk burning himself to death because of his government's supposed pro-Catholic policies. A Czech student used this protest against Russian invasion.

▲ **Heroes of the New Left** paraded by German marchers: Karl Liebknecht (shot after leading a left-wing revolt in Berlin, 1919); Ho Chi Minh of North Vietnam; Che Guevara; Lenin, leader of the 1917 Russian Revolution; and Rosa Luxembourg, co-leader of the 1919 revolt.

INFORMATION LIBRE

▲ **"Free information".** This French poster of 1968 mocks the supposed freedom of radio and other media, in fact subject to government censorship. The New Left claimed that news was always distorted, since papers were owned by the rich, advertisers controlled commercial media, and the orthodox political parties were leagued in a conspiracy of silence.

▲ **Satirical models of Mayor Daley and "pigs".** As hostility grew, "pigs" became the standard term for policemen in American radical circles. Daley was mayor of Chicago in 1968, when the Democrats met there to choose a candidate for president. There were mass anti-war and radical demonstrations in the streets, and Daley was blamed for defending the police

brutality often used against the demonstrators.

Incidents in the "siege of Chicago" were seen nationwide on T.V. and relayed all over the world. The wide publicity given to the New Left actually stimulated it by encouraging imitation. This was also the case of student revolution (below) which spread from one country to another.

Student Unrest

1968, year of student revolution in the U.S.A., West Germany, France, Japan, Italy and Britain. Protest against "U.S. imperialism" was combined with criticism of the universities; many students felt they should have more say in the running of universities, and that changes were needed in the courses.

In April trouble broke out at Columbia University, where students opposed the military research carried out for the U.S. government. At about the same time, the shooting of a student leader sparked off violent action throughout Germany.

But the "student revolution" reached its climax in France during May and June. It began when police brutally broke up demonstrations by students of the Sorbonne (the University of Paris). Many Parisians supported the students when they took over the city's Latin Quarter, put up barricades, and defied the police. There were epic battles, and the Sorbonne was occupied in an atmosphere of intense revolutionary enthusiasm. Contact was also made with French workers, who were taking over a number of factories.

Finally the whole movement collapsed. And although President de Gaulle's authority was shaken, Frenchmen swung back to conservatism.

◀ **Japanese students** were particularly militant and left-wing, perhaps because Japanese life was still run on mainly authoritarian lines. Also, military treaties giving the U.S. bases in Japan were resented. In the clash shown here both sides are impressively well-prepared. The dark mass of riot police and the advancing students face each other like gladiators.

53

The Main Events

▲ **1960:** Gary Powers, pilot of the American U-2 spy plane, shot down over Russian territory.

▲ **1962:** good relations between India and China ended with bitter border disputes. A guard protects workers on the Chinese side.

▲ **1967:** the U.S. was bitterly divided over the Vietnam war. Here a shop sign warns off those who refused army service.

1960
February: British prime minister Harold Macmillan makes "wind of change" speech at Cape Town. At Sharpeville, South Africa, 67 Africans shot by police during demonstrations against the pass laws.
May: U-2 spy plane shot down over Russia. Quarrels over the incident wreck Paris summit talks. European Free Trade Area (E.F.T.A.) formed. Adolf Eichmann, wartime Gestapo chief in charge of liquidating Jews, captured in Argentina and taken for trial to Israel. Turkish government overthrown.
June: anti-U.S. student riots in Japan; President Eisenhower postpones his visit. Former Belgian Congo becomes independent.
July: Congolese army mutiny begins years of strife; province of Katanga breaks away.
August: Cyprus becomes independent republic. Much of French Africa independent.
November: Kennedy wins U.S. presidential election.
General
Bathyscaphe *Trieste* reaches deepest point of ocean bed, Challenger Deep in Pacific.
First lasers made.
Book: Updike, *Rabbit Run*. Play: Pinter, *The Caretaker*. Films: Fellini, *Dolce Vita*, Antonioni, *L'Avventura*.

1961
January: Congo: murder of former premier Lumumba. John F. Kennedy takes office.
March: Kennedy establishes U.S. Peace Corps for voluntary work overseas. Russia puts first man into space (Gagarin). Bay of Pigs, Cuba, invaded by exiles. Algeria: army revolt against de Gaulle's policy fails.
May: South Africa becomes republic and leaves Commonwealth.
August: Britain applies for Common Market membership. East Germans build the Berlin Wall.
September: Syria breaks up union with Egypt (U.A.R.).
December: Indian forces take over Portuguese colony of Goa. Katanga reunited with Congo after U.N. intervenes. Eichmann found guilty and sentenced to death.
General
Structure of D.N.A. (deoxyribonucleic acid), basic genetic material, discovered.
New Testament of New English Bible (translation into modern English) published.
Book: Richard Hughes: *Fox in the Attic*. Play: Whiting, *The Devils*. Revue: *Beyond the Fringe*. Film: Truffaut's *Jules at Jim*. Music: Britten, *Midsummer Night's Dream*.

1962
March: cease-fire in Algeria.
April: West Indies Federation breaks up.
May: Eichmann hanged.
July: Algeria independent. Britain: Commonwealth Immigrants Act limits immigration from West Indies, Pakistan, etc. Telstar, first communications satellite, in orbit.
August: Jamaica and Trinidad and Tobago independent.
October: Cuban missile crisis. Opening of Vatican Council to discuss problems of Roman Catholic Church. Uganda independent.
December: Russo-American agreement on peaceful use of outer space. Tanganyika independent.
General
Border war between India and China.
Anglo-French agreement to build Concorde.
Medical drug, Thalidomide, taken by pregnant women, results in many malformed babies.
Opening of new Coventry Cathedral.
Satire boom in Britain: magazine *Private Eye*, T.V. programme *That Was The Week That Was*.
Book: Solzhenitsyn, *A Day in the Life of Ivan Denisovich*. Play: Albee, *Who's Afraid of Virginia Woolf?*

1963
January: de Gaulle vetoes British entry into Common Market after almost two years of talks.
June: Britain: Profumo (War Minister) resigns over sex and security-leak scandal. Valentina Tershkova (U.S.S.R.) first woman in space. U.S.A.-U.S.S.R. "hot line" between Washington and Moscow.
July: devastating earthquake at Skoplje, Yugoslavia. Britain: Peerage Act allows peers to renounce titles and sit in House of Commons.
August: nuclear test-ban treaty between U.S., Russia and Britain.
September: Federation of Malaysia formed.
November: U.S. president Kennedy assassinated; the assassin, Lee Harvey Oswald, later shot by Jack Ruby. Vice-President L. B. Johnson becomes president.
December: Kenya and Zanzibar independent.
General
"Beatlemania" sweeps Britain and later U.S.
Break-up of Central African Federation.
Book: Günter Grass, *The Tin Drum*. Play: Hochhuth, *The Representative*. Film: Ingmar Bergman, *The Silence*. Music: Britten, *War Requiem*. Controversy over Bishop of Woolwich's book *Honest to God*.

1964
April: Tanzania formed from Tanganyika and Zanzibar.
May: Egypt's Russian-built Aswan Dam opened.
July: Malawi (ex-Nyasaland) independent. Race riots in Harlem, New York.
September: Malta independent.
October: Russia: fall of Khrushchev; Brezhnev and Kosygin take over as first secretary of Communist Party and prime minister. China explodes atomic bomb. Zambia (ex-Northern Rhodesia) independent.
November: Johnson re-elected U.S. president.
General
Landings of Indonesian troops in Malaysia.
Warren Report on Kennedy's assassination.
Britain: Labour government led by Harold Wilson; beginning of "incomes policy" to hold back inflation.
Britain: Violence between Mods and Rockers at seaside resorts.
BBC2, third British television channel, opened.
Books: Saul Bellow, *Herzog*; William Burroughs, *The Naked Lunch*; Gore Vidal, *Julian*; J. P. Sartre, *Words*. Play: Arthur Miller, *After the Fall*. Films: Peter Brook, *Lord of the Flies*; Stanley Kubrick, *Dr Strangelove*.

1965
February: U.S. begins bombing of North Vietnam.
March: astronaut Alexey Leonov makes first space walk. Britain: National Board for Prices and Incomes set up.
April: civil war in Dominican Republic.
May: Southern Rhodesia: Ian Smith's Southern Rhodesian Front wins sweeping election victory. U.S. intervenes in Dominican Republic.
July: Britain: Edward Heath becomes leader of the Conservative Party in opposition.
August: Singapore leaves Federation of Malaysia.
September: British government's "National Plan" for economic growth, later abandoned.
October: failure of Communist coup in Indonesia; massacres of Communists and beginning of the end for President Sukarno.
November: Southern Rhodesia declares U.D.I.— unilateral (one-sided, i.e. without British agreement) declaration of independence; denounced as illegal by British government. India and Pakistan at war. General Mobutu takes power in the Congo; beginning of stabilisation.

1966

January: India and Pakistan sign peace agreement at Tashkent, U.S.S.R.
February: Russia's Luna 9 makes "soft" Moon landing; writers Sinyavsky and Daniel sentenced to prison for publishing works abroad. Ghana: Nkrumah overthrown.
March: Negro riots in Watts, Los Angeles.
May: Guyana (ex-British Guiana) independent.
June: Indonesia-Malaysia "confrontation" ends.
July: Negro riots in Chicago, Cleveland, Brooklyn. General Gowon takes power in Nigeria.
September: South African prime minister Verwoerd assassinated. Negro riots in San Francisco.
October: Lesotho (ex-Basutoland) independent.
November: Barbados independent.
General
Beginning of China's Cultural Revolution.
Fears aroused by successes of N.D.P., allegedly "neo-Nazi" party in West Germany.
South Vietnam: fighting between army and Buddhists.
U.S. H-bomb lost off Spanish coast for 80 days.
Book: Barth, *Giles Goat-Boy*. Films: Reisz, *Morgan, A Suitable Case for Treatment*.

1967

January: U.S.A., U.S.S.R. and U.K. sign treaty banning nuclear weapons in outer space. Coup in Togo.
February: treaty to keep nuclear weapons out of Latin America.
March: Indonesia: Sukarno loses remaining powers to General Suharto.
April: army coup in Greece.
May: de Gaulle vetoes British membership of Common Market. Biafra breakaway from Nigeria.
June: Israeli victory in Six-Day War. Negro riots in several U.S. cities. First Chinese H-bomb.
September: Gibraltar votes to keep links with U.K.
October: Che Guevara killed in Bolivia.
December: Greek king's counter coup fails; flees to Italy. Cape Town: first heart transplant.
General
Intense terrorism in Aden wins independence.
Liner *Queen Elizabeth II* launched.
U.K.: reform of laws on abortion and homosexuality.
Book: Malraux, *Antimemoirs*. Play: Stoppard, *Rosencrantz and Guildenstern Are Dead*.

1968

January: Dubcek becomes Czech leader.
March: Commonwealth Immigrants Act limits immigration into U.K.
April: U.S.: Martin Luther King assassinated. West Germany: riots after student leader Rudi Dutschke shot. Race Relations act against discrimination (U.K.); Civil Rights Act (U.S.). Student sit-in at Columbia University.
May: student-worker "revolution" in France (to mid June).
June: Robert Kennedy assassinated. Overwhelming Gaullist victory in French elections. Student demonstrations in Yugoslavia.
July: treaty to stop spread of nuclear weapons.
August: Russians and allies invade Czechoslovakia. Demonstrations and violence at Chicago Democratic Party convention.
October: U.S. halts bombing of North Vietnam.
General
Civil Rights movement in Northern Ireland.
Theatre censorship abolished in Britain.
Book: Watson, *The Double Helix*. Theatre: *Hair*.
Films: Kubrick, *2001*; Nichols, *The Graduate*.

1969

January: Nixon becomes U.S. president. 4-way Vietnam peace talks in Paris.
February: Arab terrorists attack Israeli airliner at Zurich.
March: fighting on Russo-Chinese border.
April: Czechoslovakia: Dubcek loses leading position; ousted completely later in year. De Gaulle resigns after defeat in referendum.
June: Georges Pompidou French president.
July: Apollo 11 mission: first men on Moon.
August: France devalues franc.
October: Willy Brandt West German chancellor.
General
End of China's Cultural Revolution.
Nationwide demonstrations against Vietnam war in U.S.
U.S. troop withdrawals and "Vietnamisation" begin.
U.S.: Senator Edward Kennedy, brother of John and Robert Kennedy, involved in police investigations following drowning of girl staff member in his car.
Books: Roth, *Portnoy's Complaint*; Nabokov, *Ada*.

▲ **1968:** thousands starved during the Nigerian civil war. Biafran children queue for coconut.

▲ **1968:** barricades in Paris's Latin Quarter, raised by students against the police.

▲ **1969:** Mick Jagger of the Rolling Stones, performing to a huge audience in Hyde Park, London

Adenauer, Konrad (1876-1967). West German leader. He had been Lord Mayor of Cologne before the war, and was twice imprisoned by the Nazis. In 1946 he became chairman of the newly founded political party, the Christian Democratic Union. In 1949, when the Christian Democrats won West Germany's first post-war election, Adenauer became Chancellor. He committed West Germany to N.A.T.O. and conciliated France. He held power for 14 years, resigning in 1963.

Ali, Muhammed (1942-). Black U.S. boxer, known as Cassius Clay until converted to the Black Muslim sect. He became world heavyweight champion in 1964 by beating Sonny Liston, but was later deprived of the title after refusing to serve in the U.S. army. Later (1974) he regained the title.

Barnard, Dr Christiaan (1922-). South African surgeon; he studied in South Africa and the U.S. He developed a new kind of artificial heart valve, and then experimented on transplantation of dogs' hearts. In 1967 he performed the first human heart transplant, using the heart of an accident victim.

Beatles, The. British pop group: George Harrison (1943-), Paul McCartney (1942-), John Lennon (1940-1980), Ringo Starr (1940-). All were from Liverpool, a great pop centre of the sixties. The group was formed in 1960 and leaped to fame in 1962-3. The Beatles experimented more freely than most pop artists, ranging from Rock 'n' Roll to the highly original *Sergeant Pepper's Lonely Hearts Club Band*. The group broke up in 1971.

Brandt, Willy (1913-). German politician, leader of the Social Democrats. His real name was Karl Herbert Frahn; he changed it to Willy Brandt while in Scandinavian exile during the Nazi period. As mayor of West Berlin from 1957 he strongly resisted East German pressure. He was West German Foreign Minister from 1966, and Chancellor from 1969 to 1974.

Brezhnev, Leonid Illych (1906-1982). Russian leader, an engineer who worked his way up through the Communist Party. In the fifties closely associated with Khrushchev, whom he replaced in 1964 as First Secretary of the Soviet Communist Party, while Alexy Kosygin replaced Khrushchev as Premier.

Carmichael, Stokely (1942-). Black American leader. He was born in Trinidad and came to the U.S. as a child. As a civil rights worker he soon came to believe that Negroes would only gain full equality if they were prepared to fight for it. He popularized the slogan "Black Power!"

Castro, Fidel (1926-). Cuban revolutionary and national leader. He studied law, then (1953) led an attack on an army barracks. Despite its failure, this made Castro a revolutionary hero. After three years of guerrilla warfare, he entered Havana in triumph (January 1959). His exact political stance was doubtful at first, but after quarrels with the U.S., Cuba became openly Communist.

Dayan, Moyshe (1915-1981). Israeli general and politician. He was imprisoned by the British (then ruling Palestine) but later fought with them against the Vichy French in World War Two; he lost an eye and adopted his famous eyepatch. As chief of staff he planned the 1956 Suez War; later he was Minister of Agriculture and, from 1967, Minister of Defence (to 1971), directing the Six-Day War.

Dubček, Alexander (1921-). Slovak Communist politician. He spent part of his childhood in Russia and worked in the Czechoslovak resistance movement in World War Two. He became head of the Slovak Communist Party (1963) and then of the whole Czechoslovak party (1968). His liberal policy was checked by the Russian invasion. He lost office in 1969, was sent as ambassador to Turkey, and then completely disgraced.

Gaulle, Charles de (1890-1970). French soldier and politician. In 1940, when France capitulated to the Germans, de Gaulle led the "Free French" who determined to fight on in exile. Despite his great prestige as saviour of France's honour, de Gaulle's post-war presidency was brief, and he refused to serve again unless given much wider powers. After years of waiting, his chance came in 1958 (page 24).

Goldwater, Barry (1909-). U.S. Republican politician notable for extreme conservative views. He was senator for Arizona from 1953 to 1964, and again from 1969; the gap occurred when he ran for President—unsuccessfully—against Johnson.

▲ **Fidel Castro,** leader of revolutionary Cuba.

Guevara, Ernesto "Che" (1928-67). Argentinian revolutionary; a doctor. He fought with Castro's guerrillas, and held high office in Cuba, before meeting his death as a guerrilla leader in Bolivia. He became a hero, especially to student revolutionaries.

Ho Chi Minh (1890-1969). Vietnamese Communist leader. As a young man he worked in France, and helped found the French Communist Party. In 1930 he founded the Indochinese Communist Party. He led anti-Japanese guerrillas in World War Two, and then fought the French until they were driven out (1954). As president of North Vietnam during the U.S. bombing, Ho became an internationally-known figure.

Johnson, Lyndon Baines (1908-73). U.S. politician. As Vice-President (1960-3) he had little power, but Kennedy's assassination made him President, and he was re-elected by an unprecedented majority in 1964. Distinguished for medicare, civil rights and other reforms, his administration foundered on its Vietnam policy.

Kennedy, John F. ("Jack") (1917-63). U.S. politician; his father made a large fortune in business and was Ambassador to Britain. Kennedy served with distinction in World War Two, then became a Congressman (1947-53) and Senator (1953-61). Elected President (1960), he had to deal with the Berlin and Cuba crises. He set up the Alliance for Progress and the Peace Corps, but at home most of his reforms were blocked in Congress. His assassination in Dallas shocked the world.

Kennedy, Robert F. ("Bobby") (1925-68). U.S. politician, brother of John F. Kennedy. He was Attorney General (1961-4), a Senator (1964-8), and would probably have run for President in 1968, when he was assassinated at a meeting.

Kenyatta, Jomo (1894-1978). Kenyan politician, President of the Kenya African Union (1947). He was arrested (1952) and imprisoned as supposed manager of the terroristic Mau-Mau secret society. On independence he became Premier of Kenya.

King, Martin Luther (1926-68). U.S. Negro leader. A Baptist minister of Montgomery, Alabama, King led a boycott of the segregated bus system (1956). His Southern Christian Leadership Conference became the spearhead of a mass campaign of non-violent protest. His influence seemed to be declining, and he was planning new tactics when he was assassinated.

▲ **The Beatles:** George, John, Paul and Ringo.

Kosygin, Alexey Nikolayevich (1904-). Russian politician who succeeded Khrushchev as Prime Minister on the latter's fall (1964). Kosygin and Brezhnev thus held the leading positions in Russia, but Brezhnev was generally supposed the more powerful.

Khrushchev, Nikita Sergeyevich (1894-1971). Russian politician who took power soon after Stalin's death in 1953. In 1956 he denounced Stalin's terror and began a more liberal policy. More consumer goods were produced, but Khrushchev's agricultural policy failed. Abroad, he adopted a policy of "peaceful coexistence" with the West, breaking with Russia's one-time ally China.

Leary, Timothy (1920-). U.S. professor of psychology at Harvard who argued that L.S.D. and similar drugs were beneficial if taken under the right controls. He was dismissed and later imprisoned but escaped abroad.

Macmillan, Harold (1894-). Skilful British politician, nicknamed "Supermac", who presided as Prime Minister over the boom of the late fifties; he won the 1959 election on the slogan "you've never had it so good". The last years of his government were marred by scandal, and by Britain's failure to be accepted into the Common Market.

▲ **Moshe Dayan,** Israeli defence chief.

Mao Tse-tung (1893-1976). Chinese Communist leader since the thirties. After the Communist victory over the Nationalists in 1949, the new China took shape under Mao's guidance, but in 1959 he lost some authority after failures in industrialization. The Cultural Revolution (1966-9) made him even more powerful than before, and showed his undiminished radicalism.

Nasser, Gamal Abdul (1918-70). Egyptian soldier and politician who ousted the previous military leader, General Neguib, in 1955. Nasser embodied hopes for Arab unity and socialism, as opposed to the traditional Arab monarchies. Despite disastrous defeats by Israel, his death was mourned by all Egypt.

Nixon, Richard Milhous (1913-). U.S. politician, vice-president under Eisenhower (1953-61). He was narrowly defeated by Kennedy in the presidential election of 1960, but made a come-back to win in 1968; he ordered the withdrawal of U.S. troops from Vietnam. Re-elected in 1972, scandal ("Watergate") forced his resignation in mid-term (1974).

▲ **Kennedy and Nixon,** political rivals.

Nkrumah, Kwame (1909-72). Ghanaian politician. Trained as a lawyer, Nkrumah led the movement for self-government for the Gold Coast; he was Prime Minister, 1952-7, and then when it became independent as Ghana. As President (from 1960) he became increasingly dictatorial until his government was overthrown by an army coup while he was in China.

Nyerere, Julius (1921-). Tanzanian leader. Originally a teacher, he founded and led T.A.N.U. (Tanganyika African National Union). After independence he was Prime Minister (1961-2) and President (1962-4). He became head of state when Tanganyika and Zanzibar united as Tanzania, following more left-wing policies than most African states.

Ojukwu, Chukwuemeka (1933-). British-trained Nigerian soldier. In 1966 he became Military Governor of Eastern Nigeria, the territory of the Ibo. In 1967 he declared the region independent as Biafra, ruling until its fall in 1970.

Pele, Edson Arantes do Nascimento (1937-). Brazilian footballer, recognized as the outstanding player of the sixties. He was the only footballer to win three World Cup medals (1958, 1962, 1970). He played for Brazil 110 times, retiring in 1971.

Pompidou, Georges (1911-74). French politician who came to prominence as a follower of de Gaulle. He was Prime Minister from 1962 to 1968, and on de Gaulle's resignation became President (1969). His policies were more flexible than de Gaulle's; he devalued the franc and welcomed the enlargement of the Common Market to include Britain and other E.F.T.A. countries.

Powell, Enoch (1912-). British politician; Minister of Health in the Conservative government, 1960-3, but often at odds with the party leaders over economic policy. From 1967 he made anti-immigration speeches that many regarded as appealing to racial prejudice, gaining some popular following.

Quant, Mary (1934-). British dress designer who played a key role in sixties fashions. In 1957 she opened a boutique called "Bazaar" in the King's Road, Chelsea (London). Her designs for mini-skirts, ankle strap shoes, shiny coats and boots, etc. were so popular that eventually there were hundreds of branches of her shops, also selling make-up, etc.

Smith, Ian (1919-). Rhodesian politician. He served in the R.A.F. and then farmed in Rhodesia before going into politics. He was a founder of the Rhodesian Front (1962), and after its election victory became Deputy Premier. In 1964 he became Prime Minister, representing those who preferred to break with Britain rather than yield on the issue of white supremacy. He declared independence (U.D.I.) in 1965, successfully defying Britain and the U.N.

Tshombe, Moïse (1919-69). Congolese politician who in July 1960 led Katanga, the richest province, in a breakaway from the Congo, backed by Belgian and white mercenary support. After intervention by U.N. forces Katanga was reunited with the Congo, and Tshombe fled to Spain (January 1963). He returned briefly (1964-5) as Congo premier, went into exile again, and was kidnapped and held in Algeria until his death.

Verwoerd, Hendrik (1901-66). South African politician; born in Holland. He was a professor of applied psychology, a political journalist, and then in 1950 Minister for Bantu Affairs. As such he was responsible for apartheid (separation of races) policies, which he also pursued as Prime Minister (from 1958). In 1961 he took South Africa out of the Commonwealth. He was assassinated in parliament.

Warhol, Andy (1931-). U.S. artist important in the development of the Pop Art movement; previously a commercial designer. His typical works are silk-screen prints, e.g. the Marilyn Monroe series; unlike conventional paintings these could be produced in numerous copies. In recent years Warhol has made underground films which are many hours long, or performed by non-professionals, etc.

Wilson, Harold (1916-). British Labour politician; President of the Board of Trade, 1947-51. Although associated with left-wing opposition to party leader Gaitskell, Wilson became leader on Gaitskell's death in 1963, and succeeded in uniting the party. As Prime Minister, 1964-70, his policies to encourage growth and check inflation met with only limited success. He became Prime Minister again in 1974.

▲ **Harold Wilson,** British Prime Minister.

X, Malcolm (1925-65). U.S. Negro leader; original name Malcolm Little. He was a small-time criminal, but while in prison was converted to the Black Muslim sect. He became one of their leaders, but his emphasis on violence led to a break. He was shot down at a mass-meeting. His autobiography, published after his death, influenced black militancy.

Man and the Moon

The moon is earth's nearest neighbour. This project explains the principles which govern its movements, and man's, in space.

The choice of the moon for the first ever landing on another world was based on two main facts. It is the nearest world to the earth, being only a quarter of a million miles away, and also it is the earth's only satellite, which means that it circles around the earth and its distance away does not vary very much. In spite of this, however, the accuracy of navigation necessary had to be exceedingly precise because of the relative movement of the earth and moon.

The moon circles the earth at about 2,000 m.p.h. but the earth itself is rotating at 500 m.p.h. It would therefore be pointless to aim a rocket directly at the moon, firstly because the moon would be in a different part of its orbit by the time the rocket had travelled 240,000 miles, and secondly because the rocket would tend to travel sideways with the earth until it left its gravitational pull.

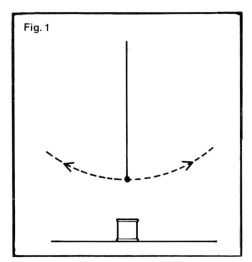

▲ To demonstrate the problems involved, tie a small weight to a piece of string about half a metre long and swing this in an arc over a small tin on the floor (Fig. 1). At the point where the weight passes over the tin, let go of the string and watch where the weight lands. In this case, the weight represents the rocket on the surface of the earth, described by the arc which it is swinging through. When the weight is released, it continues to be affected by the sideways motion and falls in an arc, as shown by the dotted line, and missing the 'moon' (your tin on the floor).

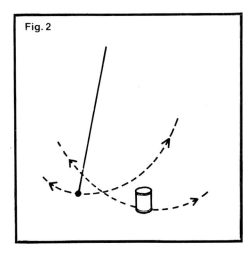

▲ Now get someone to move the tin in an arc at an angle to the arc described by the swinging weight as shown in Fig. 2. This represents the movement of the moon and makes it even harder to hit when you drop the weight. From your observations of the trajectory of the weight when released (the path in which it travels) try to estimate the point at which it should be released in order to hit the moving tin. You will notice that this is nowhere near opposite. The scientist must therefore calculate very carefully the path which the rocket needs to travel in order to be in the right place at the right time.

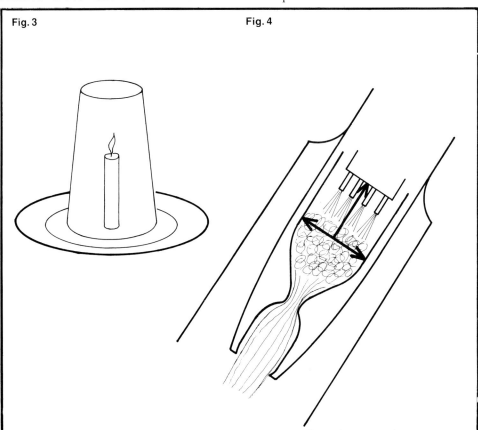

▲ The majority of engines which we use to drive transports on earth rely on combustion of various types of fuel such as petrol and oil which, when mixed with air, provide an explosive mixture to drive the mechanical parts. The air which surrounds the earth contains oxygen supplied by plant life and it is this oxygen which is necessary for combustion (burning of fuel) to take place. If no oxygen is available the fuel will not burn.

To demonstrate this, stand a lighted candle on a plate and then place an upturned glass over it so that no more air can get inside. After a few seconds, the oxygen in the air inside the glass is burnt and the candle goes out.

Because plant life is needed to provide oxygen, this gas does not exist outside the earth's atmosphere and so a different type of engine is used which carries its own oxygen supply in solid or liquid form. The fuel is pumped into the combustion chamber together with the oxygen, where they are ignited. The resulting intense heat causes the burned gases to expand very rapidly so that very high pressures are built up inside the chamber. The gases then travel at high speed through a nozzle which has the effect of propelling the rocket forward. (Fig. 4).

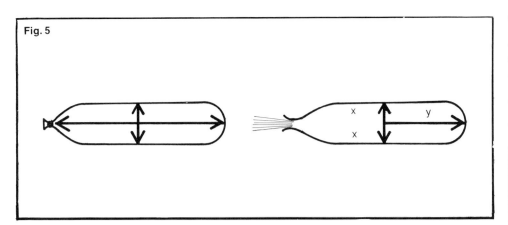

Fig. 5

▼ While the moon circles the earth, it is also rotating about its own axis in the same way that the earth does, though much more slowly, taking 28 days to complete a full turn and the same time to circle the earth. Fig. 6 shows the phases of the moon as it orbits the earth, gradually rotating so that we never see the dotted part, ''the dark side of the moon'', from the earth.

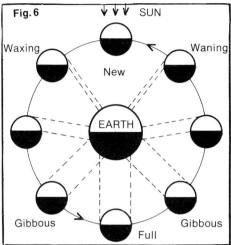

Fig. 6   SUN
Waxing   Waning
New
EARTH
Gibbous   Gibbous
Full

▲ The way in which the rocket is propelled forward by high pressure gases being ejected from the rear nozzle can easily be demonstrated with a toy balloon. Using a long balloon rather than a round one, simply inflate it as far as possible and then let it go. Note that it always travels away from the nozzle end. The way in which the escaping air provides forward thrust is shown in Fig. 5. The first diagram shows the balloon full of compressed air which is acting on all the inside faces of the balloon with equal pressure. The moment you release the air from the neck the pressure on that area drops; it still remains active on the other surfaces until all the air has escaped as shown in the second diagram. The forces 'x' acting upon the sides is still even, and so balances, but the pressure of air 'y' acting on the front surface is greater than that at the neck where it is escaping, and so the balloon travels in the direction of the greatest of the imbalanced forces.

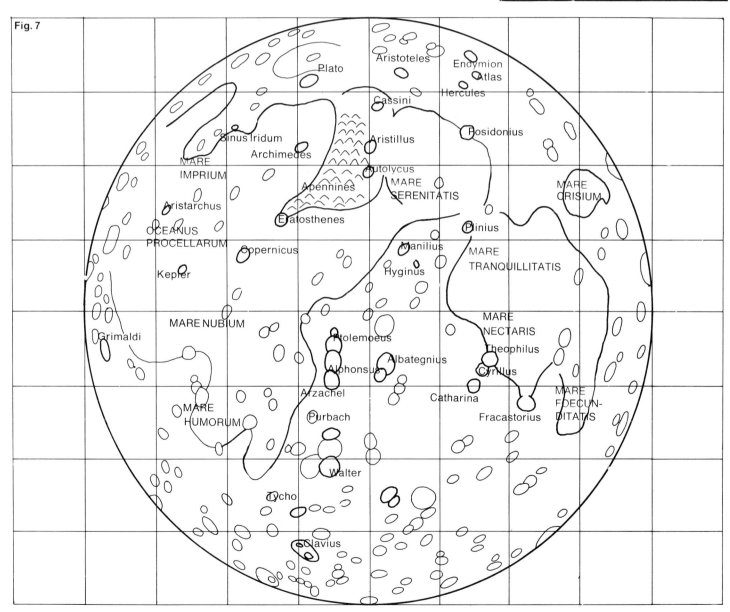

Fig. 7

▲ Fig. 7 shows the geographical layout of the moon with our names for the various areas. What appear to us as oceans are really just flat areas of land because water does not exist on the moon, but the names have been retained. From this map, try to identify the areas and find out where the lunar landings have taken place.

Using the grid lines as reference, make a copy of the lunar map at the top of a large sheet of paper, then draw a map of the earth at the bottom. Try to find out what routes to the moon have been used from different countries and plot their courses, using a different coloured pencil for each route.

Project
Op Art

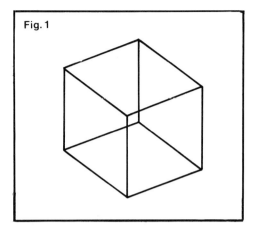
Fig. 1

"Op Art" produces an illusion of movement by confusing messages between eye and brain. Try your hand at "magic art".

Most forms of modern art rely on the observer having some knowledge of what painting is all about. It therefore sometimes becomes difficult to understand a painting when we look at it—especially if it depicts something with which we are not familiar, or if the artist has purposely distorted the way something usually looks.

During the late 1950s and early 1960s some artists were interested in producing paintings which would involve the spectator by using his eyes to make the painting 'work'. They began to create pictures which appeared to move as you looked at them. This was christened 'Op Art' (an abbreviation for optical) and was based on optical illusions which give the effect of movement by confus-

ing the eyes and the brain.

Normally, when we look at something, our eyes are able to focus on the area in which we are interested; the brain organizes the 'picture' transmitted to it from our eyes to give a realistic idea of what lies before us. To achieve this, the brain uses all the available information to build up as true a picture as possible; taking into account the relative sizes of things, their colouring, shadows, highlights and many other aspects of the visual world. Occasionally, however, the brain receives insufficient information to build up a true picture but, because it cannot 'switch off', tries out whatever possibilities of interpretation are available from information received.

Fig. 1 shows a three dimensional view of a wire frame describing a cube. Look at it for several seconds and you will notice that it appears as if you are looking at it from a higher level and sometimes from a lower one. This is because there is nothing to indicate which edge is nearest to you. Normally, we would thicken the nearest edge to us or slightly shade one side as shown in Fig. 2 to give the brain a clear indication of the way we want to describe something. This is one type of optical illusion: movement created by the brain trying things out first one way, then another, and giving a flickering image.

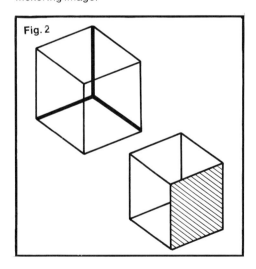
Fig. 2

A modification of this is achieved by using areas of similarity which make it difficult to focus the eye on a particular point or line because of the distraction from the similar points or lines surrounding it. Often, the picture looks stationary enough at a quick glance, but when one continues looking at it, the surface begins to move and peculiar images appear and disappear. A good example of this is the McKay figure shown in Fig. 3, which can be quite disturbing if viewed for a minute or so. Try to keep your eyes focused in the central circle and you will see how the radial lines begin to flicker and heave, trying to draw your eyes away from the centre.

Try to produce the McKay figure using opposing colours such as red and green or blue and orange instead of the black and white to see how the effect may be varied. More subtle effects on the same theme might be achieved by using slightly wavy lines of varying thickness and this too could be tried in colour.

Use bright coloured paints when trying out optical effects; fluorescent poster colours will give particularly striking effects. A fairly fine brush such as a No. 2 camel hair should be used to ensure accuracy, especially if you are working on a fairly small scale. For black and white effects it is probably easiest to draw and then fill in with black Indian ink on a good quality white cartridge paper. Do not use a smaller format than 300 mm square to ensure as much accuracy as possible, marking out the angles with a protractor or by geometric division.

Fig. 3
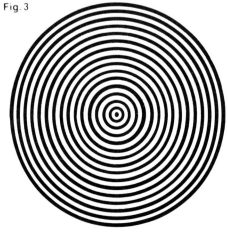

Fig. 4

Using the circle as an outer limit, it is possible to achieve effects from concentric circles. The structure shown in Fig. 4 appears to take on radial lines which revolve about the common centre of the circles and these often seem to break up the density of the black lines, making them appear as black and grey segments. Try moving the page slightly or moving your head in order to obtain a rotating effect.

Variations used on the concentric circle basis include the work of Francis Celentano and Marina Apollonio.

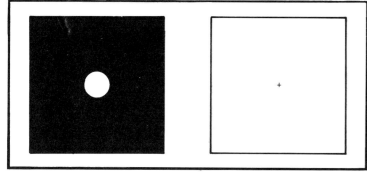

Fig. 5

Fig. 6

We look next at the phenomena of after-images, which occur quite often without our realising it. If you gaze at the white circle on a black ground in Fig. 5 for several seconds and then transfer your gaze to the cross in the adjacent square, you will see a dark spot in the centre. This is caused by the minute photoreceptors in your eyes which absorb and transmit to the brain the amount of light focussed upon them. When you see the white spot on the black square, only the receptors which see the white surface are operating and the others are in darkness. These others

come into operation when you look at the white area and the sudden change makes those already working appear darker.

The network shown in Fig. 6 uses the after image process to create dark spots where the white lines cross. If you focus your eyes on one of the crosses, the dark spot disappears and then reappears when you move your eyes to another point. The English painter Bridget Riley often uses the effects of after-images in her paintings; various shadowy images dance about the picture as one moves one's eyes.

Fig. 7

Fig. 8

Fig. 9

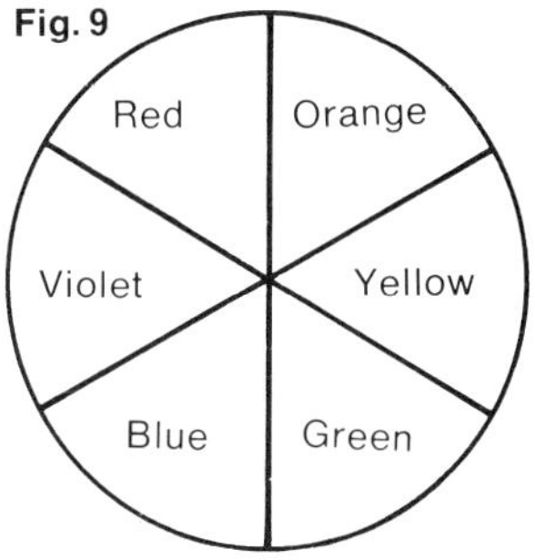

In the periodic triangle structure shown in Fig. 7, grey after-images appear to create patterns which change as the focal point of the eye is varied, often producing three-dimensional effects. When the structure is equally balanced as this one is, the variations occur in a random fashion, but more specific effects may be achieved by increasing and diminishing the height of the triangles, creating curves as shown in Fig. 8.

Try various modifications on the simple structure theme using circles, squares, varying width of lines etc. Whenever you change the dimensions of the shapes used, make the variations as gradual and as even as possible.

The effect of after-images is also apparent when using colour; the after-image of a colour is its opposite on the colour circle shown in Fig. 9. Thus, a green after-image results from saturating the eyes with red, etc.

Use one colour together with white in some of the above experiments to see what after-image effects you can obtain. When you have some idea of what can happen, try designing other combinations of repeating geometric shapes and use colour to create areas of varying interest.

Another interesting aspect of optical art is the use of the 'moire' effect. If a row of equally spaced vertical lines is overlaid with a similar row of lines placed at an angle, a pattern of curves appears as shown in Fig 10.

Even more curious effects can be made by superimposing concentric circles on a

parallel-lined base, causing circular bands of various intensity to appear as shown in Fig. 11.

If you are interested in finding out more about the artists involved in op art, the following are well-known and you should be able to obtain prints of their work from libraries or art galleries:
Victor Vaserely,   *Francis Celentano,*
J. R. Soto.   *Marina Apollonio,*
Bridget Riley,   *Miroslav Sutej.*

Fig. 10

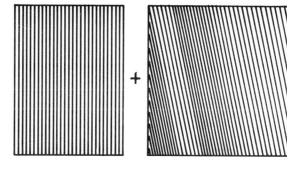

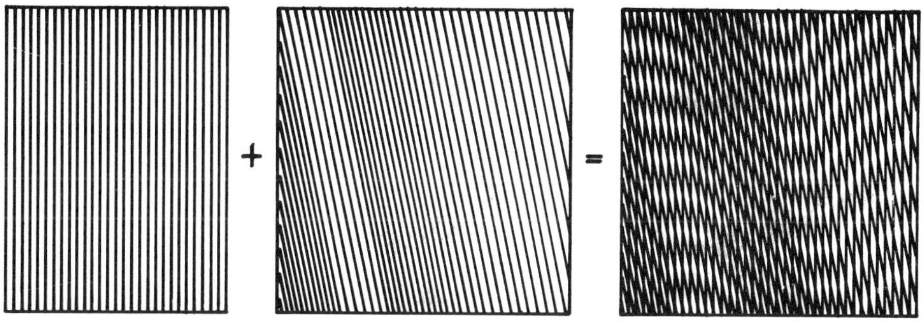

Fig. 11

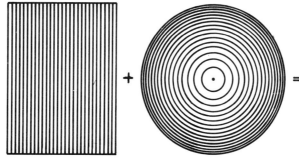

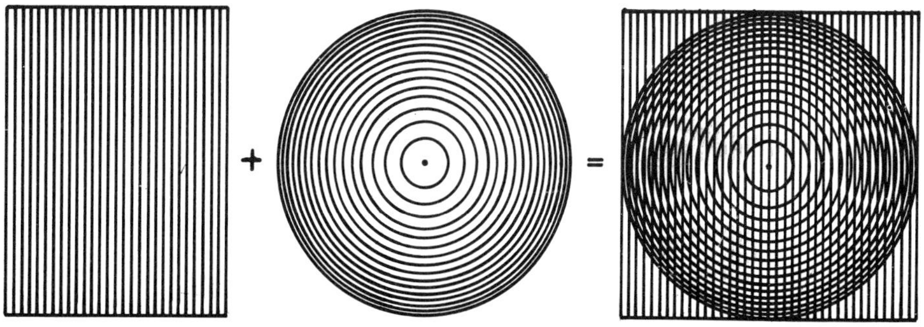

Index

NOTE: Numbers in BOLD type refer to captions.

Aden, terrorism in 55
Adenauer, Konrad, of West Germany 56
Affluence 24, 34, 38
Africa, as part of the "Third World" 30
"African socialist" state of Tanzania 11
Agricultural policy, of Khrushchev 57
Air, pollution of by industrial waste **45**
Air, travel by 34, 38
Albania, as adverse critic of U.S.S.R. 49
Aldrin, Edwin 43
Algeria **10**; independence of under de Gaulle 24, **24**
Alliance for Progress 56
"Alternative society" of youth in rebellion 15
Amateurs, banned from sporting events with professionals 20
America, see U.S.A.
Angola, Portuguese colony in Africa 10, **10**
Anti-American feeling, in Vietnam 33
Apartheid 57
Apollo II, spacecraft 43, **43**, 55
"Aquanauts" **41**
Arabs 26
Armstrong, Neil, first human on the Moon 43, **43**
Asia, as part of the "Third World" 30
Asians, in Black African states 12
Aswan Dam, in Egypt 30, 54
Atomic bombs 19
Australia 12
Austria 23
Authoritarian rule, of Charles de Gaulle 24
Authority, rejection of 50
Autobahn 38
Automation 40
Autostrada 38
Ayub Khan, of Pakistan 13

Bangladesh 13
Barbados, independence of 13
Barnard, Dr. Christiaan, and heart transplants 41, 56
Bathyscaphe, and exploration of ocean 40, 54
Batista, General Fulgencio, of Cuba 4
"Bazaar", Quant's 57
Beaches, pollution of **45**
Beatles, The, pop group from Liverpool 14, **14**, 50, **56**
Beatlemania **14**
Beatniks **14**
Belgium 10
Berlin 6, **9**, 48, 49, 53
"Berlin Wall" 6, 8, 48, 54
Best, George 20
Biafra, Ibo state in Eastern Nigeria 11, 54
Birth control, and the "population explosion" 44; and Pope Paul 51
Black Muslim sect, among Negroes of U.S.A. 21, 37
Black Panthers, militant Negroes of U.S.A. **37**
Black Power 15, 21, 37
"Blockbuster" films 35
Boats, private ownership of 38
Bolivia 5, **5**
Bond, James, a villainous hero **51**
Bonnie and Clyde **17**, 35, 51
Botswana, independence of 13
"Bottom Printing" **46**
Boutiques, in Carnaby Street, London 16; and new fashions 16
Bowling, in U.S.A. and in Europe 35

Boxing 21
Brandt, Willy **9**, **23**, 55, 56
Brasilia, new capital of Brazil 44
Brazil 44
Brezhnev, Leonid Illych 56
Britain 10, 12, 22, 23, 34, 35, 38, 39, 49, 53
British Empire 12, **13**
Brooklyn, riots in 55
Buddhist priests, in Vietnam **32**
Bull-fighting 21
Burton, Richard 35
Business, and patronage of sport 20

Cambodia **32**
Canada 12
Cape Kennedy, Florida 43
Carmichael, Stokeley, exponent of Black Power 56
Carnaby Street, London, centre for new fashions 16, **16**
Cars, pollution from 44; ownership of 34, 38
Castro, Fidel, of Cuba 4, **4**, 56, **56**
Catholic Church, rebellion in 50; and birth control 51
Catholic minority, in Northern Ireland 23
Censorship, battles over 50; of French radio **53**
Central African Republic **10**
"Che" Guevara, Ernesto, revolutionary from Cuba **5**, 50, **52**, 56
Chenpao Island **49**
Chess 20
Chicago 36; "Siege of" 53; riots in 55
Chicago Democratic Party Convention, violence at 55
China 3, 13, 18, 19, **19**, 30, 48, 49
Christian Democratic Union, in West Germany 56
Cinema 34
Civil rights movement, in Northern Ireland 55
Civil rights, in U.S.A. 8, 55
Civil war, in the Congo 10, 11; in Nigeria 10, 11, **55**; in Northern Ireland **23**; in Vietnam 32, **32**, **33**
Clark, Ossie 16
Clay, Cassius (Muhammed Ali) 20, **21**, 56
Clenched fist salute, sign of support for Black Power **21**
Cleopatra, "blockbuster" film **35**
Cleveland, riots in 55
Clothes, British 14, 16, **16**, **17**; Parisian 16
Coal, transport of 38
"Co-existence" between great powers 49
Collins, astronaut 43
Colonies 21; British 12
Columbia University, disturbances at 53; sit-in at 55
Common Market, European, see E.E.C.
Commonwealth, British 12, 13, 14
Commonwealth Immigrants Act, British 55
Communes, in China 19
Communism, in China 18; in Cuba 4, **4**, 5
Communist Party, Chinese 18; Russian 18, 47, 53
Communist Revolution, in China, in 1946 18
Communists 3, 4, **4**, 5, 6, 18, 20, 28, 32, 48, 49, 52
Computers 40, **41**
Concorde, Anglo-French supersonic aeroplane **39**, 54
Congo, Republic **10**
Constantine, King of the Hellenes 23
Contraception 51
Copper, danger of exhaustion of 44
Cornwall, England **45**
Council of Europe 22
Coventry Cathedral 54
Cuba 4, 5, **5**, 8, 49, 54
Cultural Revolution, in China in 1966 18
Czechoslovakia 28, **28**, 48, 55

Daley, Mayor of Chicago, caricature of **53**
Dallas, murder of President J. F. Kennedy at 8, 9

Dayan, Moyshe, Israeli general 56, **57**
De Gaulle, Charles 22, 23, 24, **25**, 53, 54, 55, 56
De Jong 23
Denmark 23
Der Spiegel, and Pope Paul on birth-control **51**
Detroit, disturbances in 36
"Deviations" 50
Discotheques 15
Discrimination against Asians, in Black African states 12
Dish-washing machines 40
Disillusion, in new African states 11
Divorce 50
Draft cards, burning of in U.S.A. 36
Dress, of hippies 15, 16; informality of 16
"Dropping out" of society 14, 36
Drugs, experiments with 50, **51**
Dr. Zhivago 17
Dubcek, Alexander 28, **28**, 55, 56
Dutschke, Rudi 55

"Eastern look", in dress 17
East Germany 6, **21**
East Pakistan, *see* Bangladesh
Economic growth after World War II, of East Germany **6**, 22; of West Germany **6**, 22
Egypt 26, **26**, 27, 30
Eichmann, Adolf 54
Eisenhower, President 8, 54
El Cordobes 21
Electronic sounds 46
Empire, see British Empire
England 23
"Epic" films 34
"Errors", of Chinese officials 18
Ethiopia 10
Europe 3, 6, 14, 16, 21, 24, 35, 48
European Economic Community (E.E.C.) 22, 23, 24; stamps celebrating 23; "summit conference" in 1969 **23**
European Free Trade Area (E.F.T.A.) 22, 23
Export trade, services of Beatles to 14
Eyskens **23**

Farrow, Mia **50**
Fifth Republic, French 24
Finance, for sport, difficulty of finding 20
Fleming, Ian, author of James Bond books 51
"Flower power" 14, 15
Football 20, 21
Foreigners, Chinese suspicion of 19
Forests, devastation of 44
Fourth Republic, French 24
Frahn, Karl Herbert, *see* Brandt, Willy 56
Franc, French, devalued 55
France 10, 22, 23, 24, 39, 49, 52, 53
Free French, during World War II 56
Freeways 38
From Russia With Love (James Bond film) 51
Frontier disputes, between U.S.S.R. and China **49**, 55

Gagarin, Yuri, astronaut 42, **42**, 54
Gaitskell, Hugh 57
Gambia, The, Independence of 13
Gandhi, Indira, Prime Minister of India **13**
Gang fights 17
"Gangster look" **17**, **34**
Gas, under the sea 41
Genet, Jean 46
"Gentlemen versus Players" cricket match 20
Germany 6, 22, 38, 39
see also East Germany and West Germany
Ghana (British Gold Coast) 11
Giant freight ships 38
Giant liners, decline of 38
Gibraltar, and Britain 55
Ginsberg, Allen 47
Goa, taken by India 54
Golan Heights, Syria 26, **26**
Gold Coast, British, see Ghana
Goldwater, Senator Barry 56

Golf 20
Goodyear tyres 20
Gowan, General 55
Greece 23, 54
Guyana, independence of 13
Gymnastics 21

Haight-Ashbury, San Francisco, hippy area 15
Hamburg, West German seaport 22
"Happenings" 46
Harrison, George 56, **56** (see also, Beatles)
Havana, Castro's entry into, 1959 56
Hawaii, tourists on 34
Heart transplants 41
Heath, Edward 54
"Hell's Angels" 17
Heroes, of New Left 52
Hesse, Hermann **47**
High production, problems caused by 3
Hijacking of aeroplanes, by Palestinians 27
Hippies 14, **15**, 16, **17**, 50
Ho Chi Minh **52**, 56
Holland 23
Homosexuality 50, 55
Horse races 20
"Hot line" between U.S.A. and U.S.S.R. 8
Hovercraft 38
Hussein, King of Jordan 26
Hyde Park, London 55
Hydrogen bomb 19, 48

Ibo, of Eastern Nigeria **11**
'Ich bin ein Berliner!' **9**
Immigrants into Britain 12
Independence of colonies, see Barbados, Botswana, Ghana, Jamaica, Kenya, South Yemen, Swaziland
Independence, unilateral, of Southern Rhodesia 12, 13
India 13, 34
Indian traders, in Africa 12
Indonesia 54
Industrial waste, and pollution 3, 44
Industries, and wealth 30
Informality in dress, characteristic of the decade 16
Infra-red rays, in photography **45**; in surgery 41
Instability, of French governments before de Gaulle 24; of new African states 10, **10**
Invasion, of Czechoslovakia by Russians 28, 52
Ireland 23
Iron, transport of 38
Ironworks, and pollution **45**
Isolation of China 19
Israel 26, **26**
Israeli-Arab war, 1967 26, **26**, **27**, 55
Italy 23, 38, 52, 53

Jagger, Mick 55
Jamaica, independence of 13, 54
Japan, and "student revolution" 53 **53**
Jazz, modern 14
Jerusalem 26, **26**
Jet planes 38
Johnson, President L.B. 32, 36, **36**, 54, 56
Jordan 26, **26**
Jordan, river 26, **26**
July 26th Movement, of Castro 4
"Jumbo jet" planes 38
Jupiter 40

Katanga 10, 54
Kennedy, Jackie **9**
Kennedy, President J.F. 5, 8, **8**, 9, **9**, 42, **48**, 49, 54, 56, **57**; in Berlin **9**; in Mexico **8**
Kennedy, Senator Edward 55
Kennedy, Senator Robert **9**, 36, 55, 56
Kent State University, Ohio 36
Kenya, independence of 13, 54
Kenya African Union 56

Kenyatta, Jomo 56
Khrushchev, Nikita 5, 6, **48**, **49**, 57
Kidnapping, by Palestinians 27
"Kinetic sculptures" 46
King, Martin Luther 36, **36**, 55, 56
King's Road, Chelsea 57
Kosygin, A.N. 57

Laos **32**
Laser beam 42
Latin America, nuclear weapons banned from 55
"Law and order", in U.S.A. 37
Leary, Timothy 57
"Leggy look" **16**
Lennon, John 56, **56** (see also, Beatles)
Leonov, Alexey 54
Lesotho. independence of 13. 55
Libya **10**
Liebknecht, Karl **52**
Liechtenstein, Roy 46
Life, chemistry of 40
Life Magazine, and Pope Paul VI **51**
Liston, Sonny 56
Little, Malcolm, see X, Malcolm
"Little Red Book" of Mao Tse Tung 18, **48**
Liu Shao-ch'i **18**
Liver, human **40**
Liverpool, home of The Beatles 56
Loneliness, in cities 44
L.S.D. (drug) 57
Lumumba, Patrice 54
Luna 3, 42, 55
Luxembourg 23
Luxembourg, Rosa **52**

Macmillan, Harold 10, 22, 54, 57
Maharishi Mahesh Yogi **50**
Mailer, Norman **47**
Malaysia, Federation of, Singapore leaves 54
Malawi, independence of 13; **10**
Mali **10**
Mao Tse Tung 18, **18**, 19, **48**, **49**, 57
Marat/Sade play by P. Weiss 46
Marijuana **51**
Market, in Portobello Road **16**
Mars **40**, 42
Masculine fashions **17**
Maser **41**
"Mau-Mau" 56
Mauritania **10**
Maxi-skirt 16
McCartney, Paul 56, **56** (see also, Beatles)
Medicine, and overpopulation 30
Mental illness, and loneliness 44
Mercenaries, white, in Katanga 57
Mexico, Castro in 4; Kennedy in **8**
Mexico City Olympics, 1968 **21**
Mexico, Gulf of **45**
Microwaves 41
Middle East, Russian influence in 26
Miners, in Katanga **10**
Mini car **39**
Mini skirt 16, **16**
Missiles, in Cuba 5; in Turkey 5
Mobutu, General 54
"Mods" **17**
Monorail train **38**
Moon, landings on 3, 42, 43, **43**
Moon's hidden side, photographed 42
Moscow Conference, 1960 49
Motorboats 38
Motor racing **20**
Motorways 38
Mozambique, Portuguese colony in Africa 10, **10**
Muhammed Ali, see Clay, Cassius
Musical films 34

Napalm bombs, in Vietnam 33
N.A.S.A. 9
Nasser, President of Egypt 26, 57
Nationalism in "Third World" 30, **31**
Nationalists, in China 57
Nationalisation, in Cuba 4
National Plan, British 54
N.A.T.O. 6, 24
Nazism 6
Negroes, of U.S.A. **9**, **21**, 36, **36**
"Neo-Nazi" party, in West Germany 55

Nepal, kingdom of 34
New English Bible 54
New Left 14, 37, 52, **52**, 53, **53**
Niger **10**
Nigeria **10**, **30**, 54; civil war 10, **11**, 12; independence of 13
Nixon, President Richard 32, 36, 37, **49**, 55, 57, **57**
Nkrumah, Kwame **11**, 55, 57
Noise nuisance, of supersonic aeroplanes 39
Northern Ireland **23**
North Vietnam 32, **32**, 52, 54
Norway 23
Nuclear bombs, ban on testing of 49, 54
Nuclear war 3, 5, 48
Nuclear weapons, French 24
Nyerere, Julius K. **11**, 57

Ocean bed, exploration of 40, **41**
Oil, danger of exhaustion of 44; under the sea 41; transportation of 38
Ojukwu, Chukwuemeka 57
Oldenburg, Claes 46
One-party state 10, 11, 12
Oswald, Lee Harvey, assassin of J.K. Kennedy 54
Overpopulation, in India 13; in the "Third World" generally 30, 44

Pacific Ocean **43**
"Package holidays" 34, 38
Pakistan 12, 13; division of 13; war with India, 1965 13
Palestinians 26
Paolozzi, Eduardo 44
Paris 24, 53, **55**
Parking space, lack of, in towns 39
Parliaments, in the western style 12
Pass-books, carried by black South Africans **12**
Paul VI, Pope **51**
"Peace and love" 15
Peace Corps 56
Peace, demonstrations in favour of **5**
Peerage Act, British 54
Pele, E.A., football player 57
Photography, and infra-red rays **45**
Pigs, Bay of 4, 5, 54
"Pigs" (police) **53**
Pill, contraceptive for females 50, 51
Political workers, and manual labour, in China **19**
Politics, and sport **21**
Pollution (poisoning of the earth) 44, **45**
Pompidou, President Georges 23, **25**, 55, 57
"Pop art" 46, **46**
Pop festivals **15**
"Population explosion" 30, 44
Portobello Road, London, market held in **16**
Portugal 23
Powell, Enoch 57
Powers, Garry **54**
Prague 28
President of France, powers of in Fifth Republic 24
Professionalism, in sport 20
Propaganda, national, and sport 21
Prosperity, in Paris 24
Protestants, of Northern Ireland 23
Protests, against war in Vietnam 36, **37**, **52**, 55

Quant, Mary 16, 57
"Quarantine". American, on arms to Cuba 5
Quebec Separatist Movement 12
Queen Elizabeth II, liner **41**, 54

Race Relations Act, British 55
Racial policies, of the Republic of South Africa 12
Racial problems, in the British Commonwealth 12
"Rat race" 14
"Rebellion in the Church" **50**
Records, in sport 20
Re-cycling, of the earth's used

resources 44
Red Guards, in China 18, **19**
Referenda, in France under de Gaulle 24
Refugees, from East Germany 6; Palestine 26, 27, **27**
Resistance, Czechoslovak, during World War II 56
Resources, of the earth 44
Rhine, river **39**
Rhodesia 10, **10**, 12, 13, 54
Rhodesian Front 57
Riot police, in Paris 24
Riots, in U.S.A. 36
Rockers 17
Rolling Stones 15, **55**
Rubbish, great amount of 44
Ruby, Jack 54
Rumor, Mr. **23**
Russia 3, 4, 5, 6, 8, 19, 21, 26, 27, 28, 30, 42, 47, 48, 53
"Russian clothes" 17
Rwanda **10**

San Francisco, riots in 55
Satellites, man-made 42
"Satellites" of U.S.S.R. 28
Saturn **40**
Saturn 5, launching vehicle 43
School, American, in West Germany **6**
Science fiction 46
Scunthorpe, pollution in **45**
Seabed cities, possibility of 41
Sea, transport by 38
Segregated buses, boycott of, 1956 56
Self-burning, in protest **52**
Sex, attitudes to 50; books on **51**
"Shanty towns" 30
Sharpeville, South Africa 54
Siddharta 47
Sierra Leone, independence of 13
Sinai 26, **26**, **27**
Sinatra, Frank 14
Singapore 54
"Sit-in" at Columbia University, 1968 55
Six-Day War, see Israeli-Arab War
Skoplje, Yugoslavia, earthquake at 54
Slums, in U.S.A. **9**, 36
Smith, Ian, and unilateral independence of Southern Rhodesia **12**, 57
"Smokeless zones" 45
Solar system, human knowledge of 40
Solzhenitsyn, Alexander 47, 54
Somalia **10**
"Sonic boom" of supersonic jets 39
Sorbonne University, Paris 53
South Africa, Republic of 10, **10**, 12, 54
South America 5, 30
South Vietnam 32, **32**, 54
South West Africa **10**
South Yemen, independence of 13
Space, exploration of 9, 40, 48
"Space walk" 42
"Spaghetti junctions" of roadways **39**
"Spies in the sky" 42, 48
Stalin 21
Starr, Ringo 56, **56** (see also, Beatles)
Steppenwolf 47
Stereo record players 34
Strasbourg 22
"Student revolution" 52, 53, **53**, 55 **55**
"Student-worker revolution" in France, 1968 24, 53
"Sub-atomic level", in science 40
Sudan **10**
Suez Canal 26, **26**
Sugar industry 4
Suharto, General 55
Sukarno, President of Indonesia 54
"Supermac", see Macmillan, Harold
Supersonic aeroplanes 38, 39
Surgery, use of infra-red rays in 41
Swaziland, independence of 13
Sweden 23
"Swinging Sixties" 14
Switzerland 23
Syria 26, **26**

Taiwan (Formosa) 49
Tanganyika 11, 54
Tanganyika African National Union 57
Tanzam Railway 30
Tanzania **10**, **11**, 54; independence of 13
Tape recorders 34

Tashkent, India-Pakistan Peace Agreement at 55
Taylor, Elizabeth **35**
Technology, effects of 40, 44
Teenagers 14
Television 20, 34
Telstar **42**, 54
Tennis 20
Terrorism, of Palestinian guerrillas 27
Tershkova, Valentina, astronaut 54
Thalidomide 54
Theatre, British abolition of censorship 55
"Third World" 3, 30, 44
Tiran, Straits of 26
Togo, coup in 55
"Ton-up" motorcycles 17
Tourism **34**
Town planning 44
Traffic problems 38, 39, 44
"Transcendental Meditation" **50**
Tribalism 10, 12
Trinidad and Tobago, independence of 13, 54
Tshombe, Moise 57
Tunisia **10**
Twiggy **16**

U-2 spy plane 8
Uganda, independence of 13, 54
"Underdeveloped" states 30
"Underground counter-culture" 14, 15, **15**, 47
"Unisex" 16
United Arab Republic **10**
United Nations 19, 26, 49
United States 3, 4, 5, 9, 19, 21, 24, 26, 27, 32, 33, 34, 35, 36, 37, 38, 42, 48, 49, 52, 53
"United States of Europe" 22
Unity, political, or Europe 22
U.S.S.R., see Russia

Vatican Council, 1962 54
Venus 42
Verwoerd, Hendrik 57
Vichy French 56
Vienna 49
Viet Cong 32, **33**
Vietnam 3, 8, 14, 36, 37, 48, 52
"Vietnamisation" 55
Violence 3, 22, 36, 50, 51
Vostok I 42

"Wall switches" 46
Warhol, Andy 57
Warsaw Pact 28
Watergate scandal 57
Watts, Los Angeles, riots in 55
Weather-forecasting, by satellite 42
Weiss, Peter 46
Welfare schemes, of L.B. Johnson 36; of J.F. Kennedy 8
West Berlin 6, 8
West Germany 6, **6**, 23, 24, 53
West Indies 12
Western Samoa, independence of 13
White domination, in Rhodesia 12
Wilson, Harold 12, **22**, 54, 57, **57**
Wimbledon, tennis tournament at 20
"Wind of change" in Africa 10, 11, 54
World War II 6, 12, 47
Writers, control of, in U.S.S.R. 47

X, Malcolm (Malcolm Little) 57

"Yankee" influence 4
Yardley cosmetics 20
Yevtushenko, Yevgeni **47**
Young people, necessity to protect 50
"Youth Revolution" 3, **3**, 14
"You've never had it so good" (Macmillan) 57
Yugoslavia, student demonstrations in 55

Zambia, independence of **10**, 13, 54
Zanzibar 11, 54
Zen Buddhism 14

Further Reading

Available in U.S. and Canada:
AVORN, JERRY L., et al. Up Against the Ivy Wall : A History of the Columbia Crisis. Atheneum 1968.
BISHOP, JIM. The Day Kennedy Was Shot. Bantam 1973.
CAREY, ROBERT G. The Peace Corps. Praeger 1970.
CARMICHAEL, STOKELY & C. V. HAMILTON. Black Power : Politics of Liberation in America. Random House 1968.
CLEAVER, ELDRIDGE. Soul On Ice. Dell 1968.
DRAPER, THEODORE. Abuse of Power. Viking Press 1967.
EVANS, ROWLAND, Jr. & RICHARD D. NOVAK. Nixon in the White House : The Frustration of Power. Random House 1971.
FULBRIGHT, J. WILLIAM. Arrogance of Power. Random House 1967.
Old Myths and New Realities. Random House 1968.
GALBRAITH, JOHN KENNETH. Ambassador's Journal : A Personal Account of the Kennedy Years. Houghton-Mifflin 1969.
GOODWIN, RICHARD N. Triumph or Tragedy : Reflections on Vietnam. Random House 1966.
HALBERSTRAM, DAVID. Making of a Quagmire. Random House 1965.
KENNEDY, ROBERT F. Thirteen Days : Cuban Missile Crisis. Norton 1969.
KING, MARTIN LUTHER, Jr. Where Do We Go From Here : Chaos or Community ? Harper & Row 1967.
KISSINGER, HENRY A. American Foreign Policy : Three Essays. Norton 1969.
KUNEN, JAMES S. Strawberry Statement : Notes of a College Revolutionist. Random House 1969.
LEWIS, RICHARD S. Appointment on the Moon. Viking Press 1968.
MAILER, NORMAN. The Armies of the Night : History As A Novel. The Novel as History. North American Library 1968.
MANCHESTER, WILLIAM. Death of a President. Harper & Row 1967.
ROSTOW, WALT W. The Diffusion of Power : 1957-1972. Macmillan 1972.
SCHLESINGER, ARTHUR M., Jr. The Bitter Heritage : Vietnam and Democracy. 1941-1968. Rev. ed., Fawcett-World 1972.
SIDEY, HUGH. Very Personal Presidency : Lyndon Baines Johnson in the White House. Atheneum 1968.
WHITE, THEODORE H. The Making of the President 1968. Bantam Books 1969.
WICKER, TOM. JFK and LBJ : The Influence of Personality Upon Politics. Penguin 1969.
YABLONSKY, LEWIS. The Hippie Trip. Western Publishing Co 1968.

Available in Britain (includes American works published in England):
ARDAGH, J. The New France. Penguin 1970.
BALDWIN, JAMES. Another Country. Michael Joseph 1962.
BARNES, LEONARD. African Renaissance. Gollancz 1969.
BELLOW, SAUL. Herzog. Weidenfeld and Nicolson 1961. Mr Sammler's Planet. Weidenfeld 1970.
CARMICHAEL, STOKELY & HAMILTON, C. V. Black Power. Cape 1968.
CAUTE, DAVID. Cuba, Yes ? Secker 1974.
CHOMSKY, NOAM. At War With Asia. Fontana 1971.
COHN, NIK. Pop from the Beginning. Weidenfeld 1969. Today there are no Gentlemen. Weidenfeld 1971.
GRASS, GUNTER. The Tin Drum. Secker 1963.
HASTINGS, P. The Cold War 1945-1969. Benn 1969.
HELLER, JOSEPH. Catch 22. Corgi 1969.
JOHNSON, J. B. The Vantage Point : Perspectives of the Presidency 1963-69. Weidenfeld 1972.
LAQUEUR, W. The Israel-Arab Reader. Weidenfeld 1969.
LESSING, DORIS. Children of Violence. 5 vols 1952-69.
LEVIN, BERNARD. The Pendulum Years : Britain in the Sixties. Cape 1970.
MAHOTIERE S. DE LA. Towards One Europe. Penguin 1970.
MAILER, NORMAN. Miami and the Siege of Chicago. Weidenfeld 1968.
The Armies of the Night. Weidenfeld 1968.
Why are we in Vietnam ? Weidenfeld 1969.
A Fire of the Moon. Weidenfeld 1970.
MALAMUD, BERNARD. The Natural. Eyre and Spottiswoode 1963. The Fixer. Eyre and Spottiswoode 1966.
NAIPAUL, V. S. A House for Mr Biswas. Andre Deutsch 1961.
NETTL, J. P. The Soviet Achievement. Thames & Hudson 1969.
NUTTING, ANTHONY. Nasser. Constable 1972.
PALMER, A. The Lands Between : A History of East-Central Europe. Weidenfeld 1970.
SOLZHENITSYN, ALEXANDER. Cancer Ward. Bodley Head 1968. The First Circle. Collins 1968.
WHEELWRIGHT, E. L. & McFARLANE BRUCE. The Chinese Road to Socialism. Penguin 1973.
WHITE, THEODORE H. The Making of the President 1964. Cape 1965.
WILSON, HAROLD. The Labour Government 1964-1970. Weidenfeld 1971.
WOLFE, TOM. The Kandy-Kolored Tangerine Flake Streamline Baby. Cape 1966. Radical Chic. Cape 1971.

Acknowledgements

We wish to thank the following individuals and organizations for their assistance and for making available material in their collections.

Key to picture positions:
(T) top : (C) centre : (L) left ; (B) bottom : (R) right and combinations : for example (TC) top centre.

Aero Exploration p. 39(TR)
Aero Films p. 45(TL)
Almasy, Paul p. 44(BR)
B.A.C. p. 39(TL)
Barnaby's p. 20(L)
Blume, Jochen p. 21(T)
Camera Press p. 8, 11(T), 13(BL), 18(BL), 37(B), (Anthony Howarth) 12(T), (Peter Townend) 21(BL), (William Vandivert) 42(B), (Michael Maren) 55(B)
Camera Press/Orion Press, Tokyo, p. 52-3
Cash, J. Allen p. 22(R)
Central Press p.51(BR), 55(C), 57(L)
China Pictorial p. 48(B)
Colour Library International p. Title page
Daily Express (Cummings) p. 22(L)
Der Spiegel p. 51(TR)
Dorfmann, Elsa p. 47(TR)
dpa Frankfurt p. 6(L)
Editions Alecto p. 44(TL)
E.M.I. p. 41(BR)
Fleischer, Nat p. 21(BR)
Gibbons, Stanley p. 23(R)
Hatchett's p. 15(TL)
Heliodore Torrente p. 5(BL)
Herblock p. 49(TR)
Holt/Reinhardt/Winston p. 47(BR)
Hoverlloyd p. 38(T)
Japanese Information Centre p. 38(B)
Jean Rey/Holmes Lobel p. 24(B)
Jochinson Ltd., John p. 41(BL)

Jung, Joachim G. p. 9(TR)
Kerlee, Charles p. 35(B)
Keystone Press p. 23(BL), 27(B), 36(T), 41(TL). 45(TR)
Kobal Collection p. 35(TR), 51(B)
Krausher, Leo p. 46(BL)
Krokodil p. 23(TL)
Le Canard Enchaine p. 25
Loma Linda University p. 40(R)
London Express & News Feature Service p. 52(BL)
Macdonald (Ed Harriman) p. 3, (Richard and Sally Greenhill) p. 19(TR), (Martin Chillmaid) p. 24(T)
Machen, Peter p. 20(R)
MacIntyre, Rob p. 15(TR)
Magnum p. 28(B), (Don McCullin) 11(BL), (P. Jones Griffiths) 33(BR), (Burke Uzzle) 36(B)
N.A.S.A. p. 43(TL), 43(TC), 43(TR), 43(C), 43(BL), 43(BR)
Novosti p. 42(T), 44(BL), 47(TL)
Papworth, Andrew p. 5(T)
Pictor p. 9(TL)
Pictorial Press p. 17(TL), 54(C)
Picture Point p. 15(BL)
Popper, Paul p. 13(BR)
Popperfoto p. 21(TR)
Private Eye p. 12(BL), 12(BR)
Punch (Brockbank) p. 39(C)
Pyke, D. p. 30(L)
Revolucion Newspaper p. 5(BR)
Rex Features p. 14(TL)
Richard Clapp Photography p. 49(C)
Romano Cagnoni Report p. 55(T), 57(R)
Simplicissimus p. 48(T)
Stern p. 34(BL), 46(TL)
Sudd Verlag p. 7
Sunday Times p. 53(TR)
Syndication International p. 14(BL), 14(R), 17(TR), 17(BL), 23(CL), 28(T), 29, 56(L)
Tate p. 46-7

Thompson Holidays p. 34(TR)
Transworld Features p. 33(TL), 37(T), 50(L)
Twentieth Century Fox p. 35(TL)
U.N.R.W.A. p. 27(T)
U.P.I. p. 2-3, 4(L), 4(R), 9(BL), 56(R), (Nick Wheeler) 33(BL)
U.S. Navy p. 41(TR)
Verlag Baermaaer & Nikel p. 50(R)
Vietnam Embassy p. 32(R)
Weidenfeld p. 47(CR)

Editor
Susan Ward

Concept and Design
Tim Healey

Project Author
Maurice Clifton

Front cover: The first man on the Moon. Astronaut Neil Armstrong takes his historic walk on July 20. 1969. Courtesy N.A.S.A.

Back cover: "I am the greatest" and "I am king" were characteristic phrases of Mohammed Ali (Cassius Clay), World Heavyweight Champion and personality of the Sixties.

Note: in this book all foreign words, titles of books, films, songs, etc. are in italics, e.g. Who's Afraid of Virginia Woolf ?

If we have unwittingly infringed copyright in any picture or photograph reproduced in this publication, we tender our sincerest apologies and will be glad of the opportunity, upon being satisfied as to the owner's title, to pay an appropriate fee as if we had been able to obtain prior permission.

64